NORTHSIDE

of
the

MIZEN

Recorded, edited and written
by
Patrick McCarthy and Richard Hawkes
Story illustrations by Thelma Ede

Dedicated to
the people of the Northside
Past, Present and Future

Published by Mizen Productions
Set by Martin Woodger at Blackdown Press Ltd.
Printed by ColourBooks Ltd. (Dublin)

ISBN 0 9536793 0 6

Cover: John J Coughlan of Lackavawn, 1997. Design & Photos by Richard Hawkes.

Acknowledgements

Many people have helped in the writing of this book with their stories, information, photographs and enthusiasm. It is the result of their interest and help and the "How's the book doing?" that has kept us at it for the past six years! We could fill the page with their names but we are indebted to:

Lackavawn: Daniel Coughlan (Kit), John Coughlan (John-J), Mary Coughlan (Kit), Jacky Coughlan (Kit), Maggie Courcey, Pat and Rose Courcey and family. Gurthdove: Patsy McCarthy (Patsy Paty), Jerry McCarthy (Jerry Paty), Bridget McCarthy, Mary McConnell, Julia Hodnett, Tommy Hodnett and Michael and Catherine McCarthy and family. Dunkelly: Sheila Brick, Charlie Bruen, Richard Collins (Allan), Tom Collins (Allan), Timothy Collins (Timmy Tim, junior), Mary Cotter (Mary Timmy), Michael Collins (Mikey Paul), Nattie Collins, James McCarthy (Jim Will), Rose McCarthy, Richard Gostyn, Owen Rich, Michael Richards, Jerome and Eileen Scully, Sister Brendan Sculley, (Clonakilty), John Scully, Pat and Ellen Scully and family, Lawrence and Jonathon Stafford, Terry Tuite.

Goleen and further afield: Bobby Allan (Toormore), Joan Barry (Clogher), Edward J. Bourke (Dublin), Jimmy Camier (Goleen), Michael McCarthy (Letter), Father Cashman PP (Goleen), Rick and Olly Collins (Balteen), John Cotter (Coosheen), Dermot and Tess Cullinane (Coorlacka), Bridget Coughlan (Ballydehob), Finbar Coughlan (Goleen), Bat Downey (Colleras), Jimmy Downey (Colleras), Hannah O'Driscoll (Prairie), John O'Driscoll (Dunmanus West), Mary O'Driscoll (Balteen), Michael MacFarlane (CCC engineer Schull), Dan Griffin (Schull), Bridget Maloney (England), Paddy Hodnett (Ballydehob), Bridie Kennedy (Dunmanus East), Betty O'Leary (Castle Haven), Kathleen O'Leary (Corlacka), Mary Mackey (Schull), James O'Mahony (Kilcrohane), Sheamus Ryan (Skibbereen), Paddy Sheehan TD (Goleen), Dermot Sheehan PC (Goleen), Finbar Sheehan (Enaghouter), Norma Sheehan (Goleen), Dinky O'Sullivan (Ballydevlin), Timmy and Mary O'Sullivan (Corran More), Jonathan Wigham (Dublin), Bernadette Wilcox (Goleen Telecottage).

Cobh Heritage Centre, Cork County Record Office, Geological Survey of Ireland, Mizen Journal, Ordnance Survey Dublin, Southern Star (Liam O'Regan) and University College Dublin, Irish Folklore.

Also our thanks to Mary Hawkes for proof reading and to Michael O'Donovan, of Leamcon, for his proof reading and invaluable translations of the Irish, and sometimes uniquely Northside words and place names.

We owe our special thanks to John Hawkes for his criticism and advice, and to Diana Hawkes and Bridget McCarthy for their constant patience and support.

A journey through time on the Northside

Preface

This book records the past ways of life; work, play and the traditions, tales and customs of the people from the Northside. It has been written from the inside looking out, rather than from the outside looking into Northside ways and is mainly in the local idiom. Some of the stories, songs and poems are known in the Parish of Goleen and other areas of the Mizen Peninsula, but many are unique to the Northside and composed to record local events.

Most of the old people had fine tales, poems and songs to recite, but one man in particular had the skill of a sheannachie. He was Patrick McCarthy's father, Jerry Paty of Gurthdove who was born and reared on Northside customs and traditions and told stories and recited local songs, many of which were handed down to him as a boy, from Thade 'Drake' Coughlan of Lackavawn. It was only after Jerry Paty's death in 1989 that it was realised what history and tales had been lost. Soon after, and late one night, sitting by the warmth of the fire, we decided to make a written record of the traditions and ways of life that were rapidly disappearing. From that time on we tried to recall what we had heard in the past and spent many happy nights gathering records from Northside families and friends and relatives.

Most of the contents of this book date from the famine times to the nineteen-sixties, but there are plenty of stories to tell from long before, and a few after these dates.

The Northsider's way of life of farming and fishing was totally dependent on the weather and the seasons and we decided that the division of the book into months was not only appropriate, but would provide the clearest and most practical way of presenting our records to you.

We are well aware that much of the heritage has been lost and that we will have made mistakes in our written research. If any kind reader can add information or photographs to 'Northside of the Mizen' we should be grateful to hear from you, and, if you are ever this way, you may be sure of a warm welcome on the Northside!

'Northside of the Mizen'
Goleen
County Cork
Ireland

Carbery

Goleen Parish

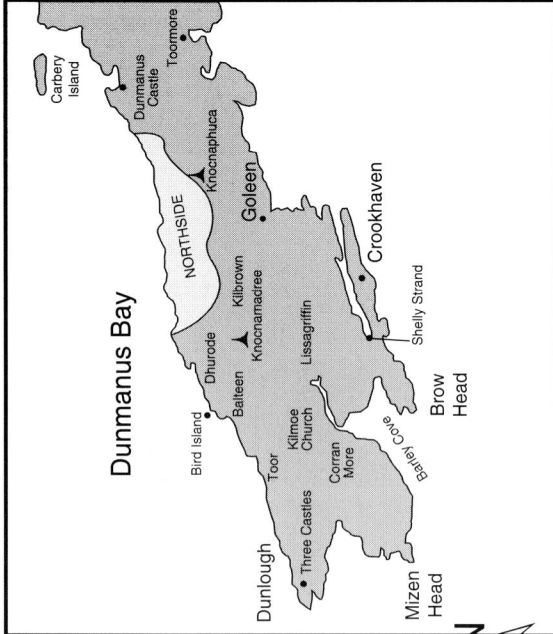

Carbery

Beara

Bere isl.

Bantry Bay

Sheep's Head (Muintir Bháire)

Durrus

Bantry

Drishane

Kilcrohane

Carbery isl.

The Mizen

Dunmanus Bay

Schull

Ballydehob

Skibbereen

Roaring Water Bay

Goleen

Cape Clear

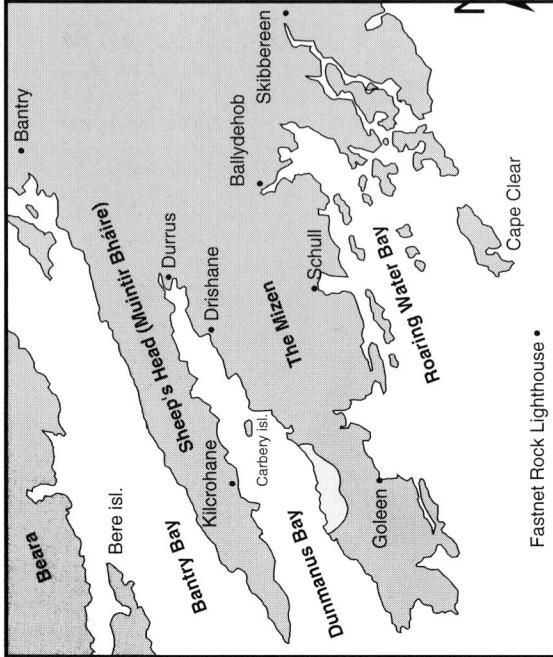

Fastnet Rock Lighthouse

Goleen Parish

Dunmanus Bay

Carbery Island

Dunmanus Castle

Toormore

Knochaphuca

NORTHSIDE

Goleen

Dhurode

Kilbrown

Knocnamadree

Balteen

Crookhaven

Lissagriffin

Shelly Strand

Bird Island

Kilmoe Church

Toor

Corran More

Barley Cove

Brow Head

Three Castles

Dunlough

Mizen Head

N

The Northside

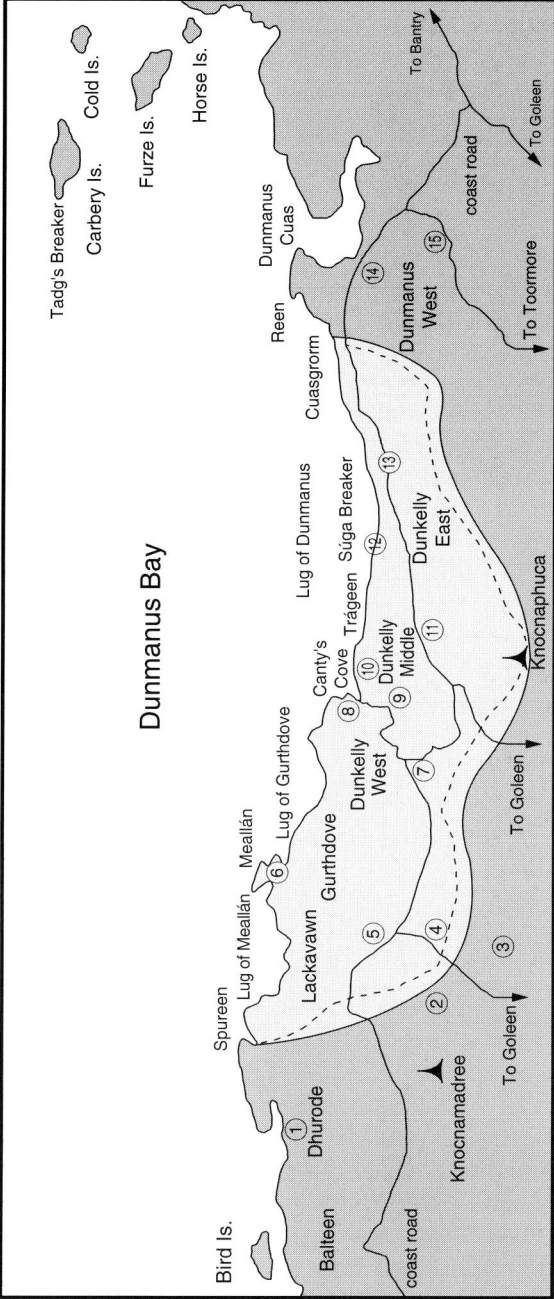

The Northside — map of Dunmanus Bay area

Dunmanus Bay

Bird Is.
Balteen
Knocnamadree
coast road
To Goleen
Dhurode
Spureen
Lug of Meallán
Meallán
Lug of Gurthdove
Lackavawn
Gurthdove
Canty's
Cove
Trágeen
Lug of Dunmanus
Súga Breaker
Dunkelly
West
Dunkelly
Middle
Dunkelly
East
To Goleen
Knocnaphuca
Cuasgrorm
Reen
Dunmanus
Cuas
Dunmanus
West
coast road
To Toormore
To Goleen
To Bantry

Tadg's Breaker
Carbery Is.
Cold Is.
Furze Is.
Horse Is.

1 Mile

① - Dhurode copper mine & fish palace
② - Bogabara
③ - Kilbrown Monastery
④ - Standing stone
⑤ - Reputed ring fort
⑥ - Meallán (Dooneen)
⑦ - Baile an Sagart (Priestland)
⑧ - Canty's ruins
⑨ - Poundland
⑩ - Killenagh burial ground
⑪ - Ring fort
⑫ - Cliff-edge fort
⑬ - Tobernasool, 'Holy Well'
⑭ - Dunmanus Castle
⑮ - Standing stone

See back of book for detailed map

Contents

'Welcome to the Northside' from Julia Hodnett

Welcome to the Northside

'The Northside' is tucked away in the remote and most south-westerly point of Ireland. It is a place of wild beauty, with hills to the back, overlooking Dunmanus Bay. In the past it offered a harsh living, where man has protected himself from the elements blown in from the Atlantic and where one person often relied on another for survival. It gave a camaraderie that can rarely be found today.

Topographical setting

The Northside lies in the Parish of Goleen (Kilmoe) on the north of the Mizen (Ivagha) Peninsula, in the far south-west of County Cork. Although the Mizen is only two miles across, the north and south are of different environments, separated by steep, rocky hills that run along the centre of the peninsula.

Five townlands make up the Northside, east to west they are; Dunkelly East, Middle and West, Gurthdove and Lackavawn, which are situated on and between the hills of Knocnaphuca and Knocnamadree with the shoreline boundary running from the Points of Reen to Spureen. The Northsiders 'home ground' out on Dunmanus Bay runs from Carbery Island to Bird Island.

View east, from The Point of Spureen

View from Reen looking west, across the Northside

History

The first settlers may well have been those from the Iron Age who developed the dun (promontory fort) at Meallán in Lackavawn, the remains of which still exist. The name Dunkelly (Ceallach's Fortress) may have derived from this fort and was the name for the whole of the Northside area in the past.

By about 750 the O'Mahonys had captured the Mizen Peninsula from the Corcalee sept and remained the lords of the land until the seventeenth century. There were at least four homesteads; ring forts at Lackavawn and Dunkelly Middle, a cliff-edge fort at Dunkelly East, all with a souterrain (underground passage), and the site of Canty's House in Dunkelly West. During this time, the upper slopes of the hills would have looked much as they do today, being above the tree line (600 feet). The lower slopes would have been forested with hazel, oak, birch, alder, and to a lesser extent, willow, pine, elm, beech and ash. The best land would have been cleared for agricultural use and the homestead.

In the early seventeenth century the Northside area was recorded as being Dunkelly (Dunnekilly) and owned by the bardic O'Canty family, who were possibly bards to the O'Mahonys of Dunmanus Castle. The O'Canty's took part in a rebellion in 1641, when they attacked Crookhaven and as a result their land was confiscated and granted to an Englishman,

Sir William Petty. At that time the population of Kilmoe was small; the 1659 census records a population of 361 people, 11 of whom came from the Northside.

In the late eighteenth and early nineteenth century the population expanded rapidly, as it did for the whole of Ireland. In 1841 Kilmoe had a population of 7,234 people of which the Northside (by then divided into the five townlands) had 117 dwellings with a population of 635. This large population managed to eke out a meagre existence in a wild environment, dependent on potato crops raised on the poor acid soils of the rocky valleys. The potato blight struck, and by 1851 the population had shrunk to 291 people in 58 dwellings, many had been evicted, but many others died through starvation in the Great Hunger.

Despite the development of employment, such as copper mining, mackerel fishing and later tourism, the population on the Northside continued to decline to 169 people in 1911. It is now at a level little more than it was three centuries ago.

Communications

Until the development of roads, the sea was the main form of communication. Crossing the hills to the south side would have been harder than rowing along the Dunmanus coastline or across the bay to Muintir Bháire (Sheep's Head). Dunmanus Bay is an inlet, and was not visited by ships on international trade routes, unlike the south coast of the Mizen Peninsula.

Before the nineteenth century the only boreen (small lane) on the Northside led from Canty's Cove to Dunmanus Castle. Later, the north coast road was constructed which opened up the Northside Townlands to the east and west. A link over the hills provided access to the south coast.

Names

Richard Collins, Richard Collins, Richard Collins, Richard Collins and Richard Collins all lived a stones throw away from each other in Dunkelly. To make life easier for themselves, all Northside families had nick names, so the five families of Collins were; the Allan's, Derby's, Paul's, Rick's and the Timmy's. Often a person would have two nick names, one for general use and the other that would not be used in front of the person themselves. These are all used in the book and we hope that you don't get confused too!

January

Bridget McCarthy, in her Northside kitchen, 1977

A new year and the cycle of passing months began again. With the weather at its worst, there was little to do on land or sea. Jobs around the home and haggard, or repairs to ditches and gaps on the farm were carried out. The house provided shelter and it was a time to be by the warmth of the turf fire for the long nights, whether at home or out scoriachting.

The New Year

January was a long, dark, bitch of a month. The weather and it's forecasting was of the uppermost importance to the farmer and his crops, and the fisherman and his safety at sea. It determined the day's events and the way of life throughout the year for everyone in the country. The old people said that if you didn't eat enough on New Year's Eve you would be hungry for the rest of the year and from whatever point the wind blew, you would get it from that point for the most of the next three months. A north or northwesterly wind, although harsh for a spell, would be a sign for a reasonably dry year. A black cat washing the back of it's ear with a paw, was a sign of bad weather and it could even mean snow. Strong, blue flames in the hearth meant that the weather was going to turn cold, but by the 21st of January the backbone of the winter was thought to be broken.

On Nollaíg na mBan (Woman's Christmas or Epiphany), the women put all the scraps and leftovers from Christmas onto the kitchen table and it was then up to everyone else to cope the best they could. At midnight, on the eve of Nollaíg na mBan, the water in the spring well turned to wine. Now that was a great thing! Ne'er a man or woman has ever supped any and that was because it was only for the little people (fairies).

The Home and Hearth

The kitchen was where it all happened in the house. It was strictly the woman's place and there wasn't a man who would get in the way. Men

and hens in those times were free range, and would roam the kitchen only to be kicked out of the house with fire tongs or brush, if they got in the way.

The big, open fire, burning in the hearth, was the centre of everything and the homely smell of the turf smoke would be throughout the house. The blacksmith made the crane that supported the kettle or three legged pot (round bastable) over the fire. Around the hob were the cake bastable (flat bastable), griddle, teapot, tongs, a small shovel and the fire machine (bellows). Often there would be fish or bacon hanging up the chimney for smoking, which, when cured, were wrapped in brown paper or fern (bracken) and hung from a beam near the fire. Above the fireplace was the clevy (mantle shelf), the driest place in the house, and it had all sorts on it; the tea, peppermint sweets, salt, playing cards, tobacco, letters from America and any other item that needed to be kept dry. 'The Sacred Heart' was a small house shrine that consisted of a Holy picture hung over a wall bracket that held a little lamp and two vases of flowers. 'The Sacred Heart' was to be found in every kitchen, usually over the settle, and, as with the fire, the lamp was always kept alight. At the opposite end of the kitchen the other great place was the dresser, with fancy plates, drinking bowls and jugs on the shelves and stored in the press (cupboard) below were cake, butter, bread, blackberry jam and other delights. Some of the houses also had

'*The Sacred Heart*'

a floor to ceiling press separated from the dresser by a door that led to the parlour. The table, chairs and settle were often made from timber taken from the sea and crafted by a local person. The settle seat usually had a flap on the front of it and you stored boots and other items there. Above the front door, between two beams, was a shelf to hold boot polish, a comb and a small mirror.

It is easy to do a man's work but a woman's work is never done! The woman of the house would be busy from the start of day. The fire was always kept red from the night before and, when rising from sleep, it was

The kitchen hearth – the heart of the home

The kitchen press and dresser with Susie at the parlour door

put into good order with the use of the big wheel of the fire machine to blow the life back into it. With the cows milked, the animals fed and breakfast provided for the man of the house and children, the baking of the cake (soda bread) was the next job for the morning. Dough for the cake was made with flour and sour-milk. If sour-milk could not be had then seawater was used in its place.

The fire was built up with plenty of turf and after a short time it would be opened up, and the bastable with the dough in it, placed into it. Turf was then put on the top and all around to give a good even heat. If the turf store was running low, dry fern (bracken) was thrown into the fire when it was opened, as this gave a strong heat. There was great skill in baking the cake, and there was nothing better to taste with home-made butter and blackberry jam. While the cake was baking the woman always had plenty of other things to do such as the clothes washing or sweeping out. Next onto the fire was the three legged pot of potatoes for the mid-day meal. They were washed and then placed into the pot with the skins on. Dry potatoes were preferred and when they had been boiled the skin would be half coming off. They were then tipped into the sciff (flat bottomed, round basket) on the table and it was time for the main feed of the day. The usual meal was made up of plenty of potatoes and milk, with a small showing of bacon or fish, and, if in season, cabbage and carrots. After the main part of the meal tea or milk and cake or bread were always had. The leftover potatoes would be given to the hens and pig, or mixed with old bread and milk for the dogs and cats.

> One bachelor, on the Northside, had a turkey that he was rearing to sell at Christmas, but, for whatever reason it was, it died before he sold it. The big turkey would not fit into the three-legged pot for boiling, so he had to boil the back end first and then he turned the turkey around and cooked the head end!

In olden times if you had a sick cow or calf, they came into the kitchen at night for warmth in the winter. This custom carried on in the bachelor houses of the Northside until the nineteen-seventies.

The parlour existed in the large single or double storey houses. It was a special room and only used for occasions like the Stations (house Mass). The parlour had a good table and chairs, a small press and sometimes a small cast iron fireplace, and they were all painted with a bright gloss paint.

In the single storey houses the main bedroom was on the ground floor, but the children slept in the loft under the thatch roof. If there was no ladder a chair was placed on the kitchen table to get up to the loft through a trap door. In the two storey houses all the bedrooms were upstairs. The main bedroom was furnished with a bed, wooden wall pegs for clothes, a big wooden box for storage and sometimes a washstand with a bowl and jug. The bed was like a big box, one plank in height, raised from the floor with sturdy legs at each corner. There were two kinds of mattress; one was made from old meal bags and filled with straw, and the other, called a tocth (mattress), was made of calico stuffed with feathers. The bed was covered with a quilt that was often sewn by the woman of the house before she was married. There were always fleas in a country house that came in on the turf; it was near impossible not to have them. In the winter the fleas were quiet but with the warmer weather they would 'draw the bad blood' from all!

> There was an old man living alone who went to the hill to bring in the cows. The fog came down and he was unable to find them. The smart lads had been at work whilst the old man was out and had put a donkey into his bedroom. The man returned home without the cows, and it wasn't long before he made for bed. As the old man opened the door of the room, the donkey came agin him. With the sound of the hooves and the cold, hairy body rubbing him, the man thought that it was the devil and he made for the front door to call a neighbour. Someone came to his call and it took some time to settle things down.

The Haggard and Outhouses

Surrounding the house was the haggard (farmyard) where the hay, turf and straw ricks stood and the fowl freely roamed. In the past the cow dung and stable manure heap was at the front of the house but for sometime now the heap has been outside the cow-house, but still within sight. The cool north linhay was for milk products with a butter churn and ceilers (large, flat based earthenware bowls), for the setting of milk, as well as hay pikes, rakes and other implements. The south linhay was for hens, turf, back-loads and other baskets. Both the linhays were lean-tos often attached to the house. Outhouses (farm buildings) were close to the haggard. There would be a double storey cow-shed or stable, and above the chamber there was a dry loft for the storing of grain and fishing nets, as well as other gear. Smaller, single storey outhouses were the pig-house and a car-house, with even smaller chambers for the geese and turkeys. Near enough everyone had a plough, and a few had a furze machine and a turnip pulper. The dogs were handy for cattle and sheep and a good dog would save a lot of your sweat. As you walked into the haggard the farm

Feeding the calves by the haggard

A two storey outhouse, with steps to the loft

dogs always gave you a good looking over and, if they didn't like what they saw, would come and smell you. It was best to let them know at that time who was boss! The cats did their own thing, and kept down the number of mice and rats.

> Hee-Haw-Haw
> The donkey's dead,
> What shall we do
> With poor old Ned?
> We'll put him in the chamber
> And give him some straw,
> And then he'll roar,
> Hee-Haw-Haw!

The blacksmiths would be busy ringing in the new year with their big hammer winging down onto the anvil. There was always a trip to the blacksmith for repairs, or to order new tools to get ready for February and the start of the farming year. There weren't any special customs or beliefs about blacksmiths in the area, but a good smith was held in very high esteem. There were forges everywhere; the Northside went to John (Jotty) McCarthy at the Masters Cross, John Hegarty at Dunmanus and Jack Dan O'Sullivan in

O'Sullivans Forge, Goleen

Goleen, who was the last blacksmith and finished his trade in 1978. There were always children watching the blacksmiths, especially when a horse or donkey was being shod.

January was a time for odd jobs around the fields and haggard, such as repairing ditches (banks) and making gaps (gateways to fields) good with a strong stick and heavy slats (large flat stones). Once in a while, a rib bone from a whale was found along the shore and used to block a gap, instead of a gate made for the purpose. One smart lad wrote on a new gate, 'Whoever made it, made it well, because they made it like the gate of hell!' And that would have been where the smart lad would have found himself, if the owner of the gate had caught him!

Feeding corn to the hens and geese and the hay from the rick to the cows, who gave little milk in return at this time of year, was part of the winter routine. The short evening and full night gave plenty of time for scoriachting at neighbours' homes and sitting by the warmth of a turf fire.

Scoriachting

Throughout the year, scoriachting (visiting neighbours) at night was the custom and in the winter the warmth of the open fire was the focus for games, songs and stories, but in the warm summer months many activities took place outside. Only Saturday was not a night for calling to friends, as you would have to get ready for Mass early the next morning. Different houses in the townlands would be known for their own form of entertainment; for example; the Coughlan's (the Kit's) for talk of people and who was related to whom, the Courcey's and the Scully's for cards, the Hodnett's for games and tricks to test your wits and for a bit of harem scarem, John Coughlan's (John-J's, the Jer Jerry's) where there'd be from pitch and toss to manslaughter!

Michael and Tom McCarthy out scoriachting

If you were a pipe smoker and you walked into a house where a man was smoking, he would offer you the pipe for a few pulls. When handing the pipe back you'd say, "The Lord have mercy on the dead." Women would occasionally smoke a pipe but preferred snuff. Often the night's scoriachting would start with the Rosary and two candles would be lit. One Sunday night in the nineteen-thirties, at the O'Donovans in Dunkelly a lad pegged (threw) a cap at one of the candles and quenched it. Danny O'Donovan said that it was a queer thing to happen in the house of God, to which the reply came, – "There's a great deal of difference between you and God!" That was the end of the Rosary that night!

A night would start with games, blackguarding (horseplay) and sometimes dancing, then progress on to songs and poems. Storytelling was the preserve of an evening by the fire. With the flames flickering and the wind and rain howling like the Banshee, the imagination of the storyteller and his forebears was let loose on a delighted and spellbound audience of children and adults alike. This, in turn, would lead to stories of a more superstitious nature, into a world of small folk, púcas (sprites), mermaids and of people's misfortune when they interfered with the fairy ways.

There are four sightings of mermaids remembered locally. In the nineteen-hundreds after a big storm, William Canty of Corran More, saw a mermaid stranded at Barley Cove. He left her alone and when the tide came in, she went back to the sea. Another time, Henry Allan saw a black mermaid stranded at Ballydevlin. He left her well alone and when the tide came in she went back to her own dimension. There is also the song 'Ever Green and Fair Dunmanus' and the Glavin story.

View over Dunmanus Castle and Bay, to Kilcrohane

Ever green and fair Dunmanus

Ever green and fair Dunmanus, o'er your hills I long to stray,
Around your shores and over where the winter was like May.
As I roamed along that quarter where the lofty castle stands,
I would swim the rippling water in your bright and silvery strand.

Where the lofty castle stands, where the lofty castle stands,
How I long to see Dunmanus where the lofty castle stands.

There's a dance in Dunmanus when our boys stepped in tiel
With the lovely country hornpipe and the sporty Bandon reel.
There was football in the Prairie there was dancing in Dreenane,
And on Sunday we went sailing o'er the bay to Kilcrohane.

Where the lofty castle stands, where the lofty castle stands,
How I long to see Dunmanus where the lofty castle stands.

You could walk the road to Scrathán[1] when the moon was shining bright,
On the waters of Tráláraigh[2] as the mermaid hove insight.
From the cove of Carrigmanus to the pier of Canty's Cove
Seines were shooting o'er the harbour down to calm Dunbeacon shore.

Where the lofty castle stands, where the lofty castle stands,
How I long to see Dunmanus where the lofty castle stands.

When the foe was in our country and our boys prepared to fight,
They would gather on the hillside as the day gave way to night.
They were drilling by the castle, where the fairies we are told
Played the sweet enchanting music in the happy days of old.

Where the lofty castle stands, where the lofty castle stands,
How I long to see Dunmanus where the lofty castle stands.

Lovely bay down by the water on your shores I long to stray,
Where the breezes o'er the harbour softly linger night and day.
When my youthful days give warning and old age is drawing nigh,
I think it'll be Dunmanus where I long to live and die.

Where the lofty castle stands, where the lofty castle stands,
My retreat will be Dunmanus where the lofty castle stands.

[1] Dunmanus West
[2] See story, The Cripples Leap (Tráláraigh).

Patrick Downey, the Glavins and the Mermaid

Many years ago in the parish of Kilmoe, near the White Strand (Barley Cove) at Lissagriffin, lived a man called Patrick Downey. He had a wife and eight children. When the time came to pay the rent to the landlord, O'Grady was his name, Patrick Downey couldn't meet the sum and the landlord, a hard man, evicted him. The neighbours, those people who hadn't headed off across the water for Muintir Bháire on account of the bad times with O'Grady, helped him the best way they could, and built a mud hut on the roadside at Carrigmanus for him and his family. It was there that the poor man just managed to keep going. The landlord then rented the Downey's house and land to the Glavins, who lived nearby at Corran More. The Glavins were a tough old crowd. There's few that would have cared to move into an evicted man's house in the parish of Kilmoe, and leave the poor man and his family on the side of the road.

The years passed by. One day, the Glavins, the father and a son, were down on Barley Cove strand collecting sand for the fields when they saw a mermaid combing her hair. She had been stranded in the stream with the tide. Half fish and half woman she was, and in her hand was a bridle. She could speak their tongue and she cried and begged from the bottom of her heart for them to put her back into the waves, but they carried her back to their home at Lissagriffin. The Glavin man hid the bridle in one of the outhouses, as without it she could never go back to the sea. The Mermaid gave great lamenting and pining for the sea, but she said that she would become a woman and marry the son on three conditions; that he must not kill a seal, that he must never eat off a sheriff's table and that he must never kill a black sheep. And so they married.

Time passed away and they had children. Years later the Glavin man went, with other men, to the sea to kill seals. He killed and skinned one. At the same time as the man killed the seal one of their children found the bridle in the outhouse and took it to their mother. She wept as she kissed her children goodbye and went for the strand. The mermaid shook the bridle at the sea and a fine white horse appeared from the waves with a saddle. She put the harness on the beast and then mounted him. As the Mermaid sank below the waves she cursed the Glavins, "Never shall seven men of the name of Glavin stand together again on the rocks of Lissagriffin". She was right. There wasn't a bit of luck for the Glavin's; they split up and died out altogether.

As the night got long in the tooth, salted fish and milk or tea and cake would be offered to the scoriachtors. If you spilled the tea or milk you would say that the little people wanted it. Sometimes food such as steampai, ríobún or yellow meal was offered. To make steampai you peel potatoes and put them through a grater until you have enough for whatever audience you have, then put it into a cloth and squeeze the juice out. Knead in flour and level the mixture out like a pancake and cook it on a griddle (or frying pan). For ríobún, you put the wheat into a pot and keep stirring it until it starts leaping out over the top with the heat of the fire. Give it half an hour or that way, then, with a hand-quern, grind out the wheat and add milk until it is like porridge. Yellow meal was brought into the country at the time of the Great Hunger as food aid. To make yellow meal gruel just boil yellow meal with milk until it thickens, and then eat away. Long ago it was the same meal that the cattle would eat, and it was also used for human consumption. You could make cake (bread) from yellow meal. It is said that since the old yellow meal went, there isn't a healthy man or beast in the country!

After the merriment, stories and refreshments, the man of the house would go out to give a pinch of hay to the cows and to settle the bed under them for the night. He'd come back in and the guests would say that they'd be pulling out. The people of the house would say "Good luck", to which you replied "Good luck to ye, now."

If the night was black as you made your way home and you couldn't see where you were going, it was a good idea to call on the little people to help you. To do this you took a piece of clothing off, turned it inside out and put it back on. That gave you the sight back and you would find your way. It was also wise to carry a twig of hazel as it would protect you from the not-so-good little folk and get you back home safely!

A man called Jerry Coughlan of Gurthdove was walking home from scoriachting from the west. He found that he was going astray. Jerry took off his gansey (jumper), turned it inside out, and put it back on. The little people came to his aid, and Jerry found that he was east off the road. He got his reckoning back and went home.

The last job at night was to build the fire up and cover it with ash, so as to keep it red for the next morning. It was bad luck to let a fire go out, and it was said that many of the hearths had the same fire for generations.

Weather lore and forecasting

Northsiders were a great hand at forecasting the weather, not only from day to day, but for the long term as well. When the wireless became affordable, in the sixties, the news and weather forecast were carefully listened to, and then discussed in depth. The advice of a Northsider, would be far better than that of broadcasted forecasts.

A good number of sayings are still known, some being superstitions and charms, while most are based on careful observation over many hundreds of years of the sea, sun, moon, sky, wind, rain, land, birds and animals. Often one man may have asked the opinion from another about the weather, and the reply could be interesting – "My goodness gracious me boy, 'tis light and dry on the bottom and breezy with a scud going bouncing beyond the moon!" Below are some sayings that the Northside people would take into account when forecasting.

The Sea

White ground siege (foam) at the shoreline means that the sea bed is being worked by currents, and it is a sign for a heavy sea. The ground siege can also appear a pink colour if there has not been a good siege for some time. The colour comes from old, rotted seaweed.

For good weather the white collar of the shore will have to leave and the shore to go down flat and blue.

If the sea is shoving up its nose or breaking at the Point of Reen, the Súga Breaker or Tadg's Breaker just west of Carbery, it is a sure sign of bad weather. A 'breaker' is where the water at the surface is broken in the shallows when the sea is running, and a 'nose' of water is a build up of water where the sea bed goes from deep to very shallow.

When you see what looks like a river of smooth water running out across the sea from the shore, it is a sure sign of rain.

If you can hear the 'out haul' (the back wash of the sea on the rocks) at Cuasathoran, it is a sign of a strong east wind. If the 'out haul' is heard at the Lug of Meallán, it means rough weather from the west or north-west.

Dried seaweed will soften when dampness is on the way.

If the brone (heat haze) is coming in from the sea, there will be plenty of warm weather.

The Sun

If there is a sun-dog (sunspot) on either side of the sun, three to four days later you will get rain.

A ring around the sun means rain, and the farther out the ring the nearer the rain.

'If the sun goes to bed pale, it is sure to rise with a wet head.'

The Moon

The weather grows (stronger winds) with the moon.

If the big ship (moon) is towing the small boat (star), it's a good sign for the weather. If there is a bright star to the left of the moon it is a good sign. If the star is to the right of the moon it is a bad sign.

If a change in the moon and the equinox meets on the 21st of September and if the day is fine it is a sign of good weather to come.

A cock's eye on the moon is not a good sign for the weather.

If the Milky Way is north-east or south-west in direction, it is a sign for good weather.

The Sky

If you see the Northern Dawns (Aurora Borealis) in the spring of the year, it is not a good sign for the summer.

If you see a madragaoth (a wind-dog or part of a rainbow), over Carbery Island in the morning, it is a sign of wind and showers.

A red sky in the morning, the shepherd's warning. A red sky at night, the shepherd's delight.

Red sky in the morning - if red is up high in the sky it will be wet in the morning. If the red stays at the horizon it could rain by mid day or if the red is up a small bit it will be a good day.

A mackerel sky and mare's tails make big ships carry small sails.

If it has been mixed weather and overcast, but the horizon is clear, the day will clear up.

If clear overhead in the morning but misty at the waterline, the day can turn to rain.

The Wind

To get good weather the wind should follow the sun; east to west. In summer if the wind follows the sun to the north-west at sundown and remains there next day it will go south-west at sunset and rain will follow the next evening. If the wind stays north all day and changes north-west with the setting sun, the following evening there will be a south-westerly wind with rain.

The small Sheegwee wind (fairy wind or whirl wind), that in the summer rises dust and hay off the ground, will be a sure sign of a good breeze and rain to come.

Scairavin na gró (Scairavin na gCuach, The Wind of the Cuckoo), is a sharp wind and showers that arrives in the middle of May. It lasts for one week or more and it was said that it was a last blast of the winter before the summer.

The Helmas wind arrives around the last week of September and with it brings the beginning of autumn.

The Rain

In the spring or the fall of the year, if you see a full rainbow on land (east to south-east), it will mean heavy weather is on its way.

> Rain on the ebb,
> Go home to bed.
> Rain with the flood,
> It'll only be a scud. (soft drizzle).

It is said that if February didn't fill the lougheens (small ponds or bogs) then May would!

If it rains on St. Swithin's Day (15th July) then you will get forty more days of rain like it.

The Landscape and House

If you can see smoke coming out of chimneys of houses at Kilcrohane, or the distant hills look near, or if Hungry Hill on the Beara peninsula has mist to the west or on it's slopes, it is a sure sign of rain.

Soot falling down the chimney, is a sign for misty, soft weather.

An old flagstone hearth will turn black with damp before rain.

Birds and Animals

'If the cock goes crowing to bed, he's sure to wake with a wetter head.'

A black cat washing the back of his ear with his paw, in the winter, is a sign of bad weather and it could even mean snow.

A cow that didn't go to the bull or a barrfhód (top sods for fuel) that isn't dry by August means that you wouldn't get either that year.

Low flying milliceens (midges) that bite you also mean rain.

If mackerel are schooling well up and down the bay, it is a sign of good settled weather.

If you see the tráheenocs (dolphins) going down the bay for Carbery Island you will have fine, dry, warm weather. If you see them going out of the bay for Sheep's Head, you'll get wind and rain and plenty of it.

If you hear a gabhairin rua (jack snipe) or the mackerel bird (auk), or see a basking shark, it is a sure sign of fine, dry settled weather.

If you see a shagga (black diver, cormorant, or a shag) going high over the land, you'll get a gale of wind, from whatever point the shagga was flying in, before the next day.

Seagulls and crows mixed together in a field is a sure sign for mixed and broken weather for up to three to four weeks. If you see a murder of crows diving like gannets, it is a sure sign of heavy rain.

If the sea gulls are calling it is a sign of a hardy, sharp wind.

If the curlew's whistle is of different notes, a change in the weather is on it's way.

Oh seagull, oh seagull
Who sits on the strand,
We'll get no fine weather
Till you leave dry land.

The Horned Woman

A rich woman sat up late one night carding and preparing wool, while all the family and servants were asleep. Suddenly a knock was given at the door, and a voice called, "Open! Open!"

"Who is there." said the woman of the house.

"I am the Witch of the Horn," was answered.

The mistress opened the door and a witch entered, having in her hand a pair of wool carders and a horn on her head, as if growing there. She sat down to the fire.

Then a second knock came to the door and a voice called as before, "Open! Open!" The mistress rose and opened the door and immediately a second witch entered, having two horns on her head and in her hand a wheel. And so the knocks went on, and the call was heard and the witches entered until twelve witches sat around the fire, the first with one horn and the last with twelve. All were singing an ancient rhyme but no word did they call to the mistress of the house.

Then one of the witches called to her in Irish, and said "Rise woman, and make us a cake." The woman searched for a vessel to bring in the water from the well so that she might mix the meal and make the cake but she could not find one. The witches said to her, "Take a sieve and bring water in it." The woman of the house went to the well. As hard as she tried the water poured from the sieve and she could fetch none to make the cake. She sat down by the well and wept. A voice came by her and said "Take yellow earth and moss and bind them together and plaster the sieve so that it will hold." This she did and the sieve held the water. The voice said again, "Return and when thou comest to the north angle of the house, cry aloud three times and say 'The mountain of the Fenian women and the sky over it is all in fire'." The woman of the house did so and when the witches inside heard the call they rushed

forth with wild lamentation and shrieks, and fled away to Slievenamon where their chief dwelled. The spirit of the well bade the mistress of the house to enter and prepare her home against the enchantment of the witches if they returned again.

First to break the witches' spells, she sprinkled the water in which she had washed her child's feet on the threshold. Secondly, she took the cake of meal mixed with blood drawn from the sleeping family that the witches had made in her absence. She broke the cake in bits and placed a bit in the mouth of each sleeper and they were restored. Then she secured the door with a great crossbeam fastened in the jambs, so that they could not enter. Having done these things, she waited.

Not long were the witches in coming back and they raged and called for vengeance.

"Open! Open!" they screamed, "Open feet water."

"I cannot," said the feet water, "I am scattered on the ground, and my path is down to the river."

"Open! Open wood and beam," they called to the door.

"I cannot," said the door, "for the beam is fixed in the jambs, and I have no power to move."

"Open! Open cake that we have made and mingled with blood," they cried again.

"I cannot," said the cake, "for I am all broken and bruised, and my blood is on the lips of the sleeping children."

Then the witches rushed through the air with great cries and fled back to the mountain, uttering strange curses on the spirit of the well, who had wished their ruin. The woman and the house were ever after left in peace.

A mantle dropped by one of the witches in her flight was kept hung up by the woman of the house as a sign of the night's awful contest and this mantle was in possession of the same family from generation to generation, for five-hundred years after.

February

Paddy Courcey and his tilly lamp, 1964

With frost and snow on the distant mountains the day's light was getting longer. As the winter gales continued, many ships floundered on the rocky shoreline of the Mizen. It was the start of the farming year, and potato ridges were dug and set as lambing got underway. The fields were ploughed for the forthcoming season. It was hard work by day and night.

St. Bridgid's Day

> If St. Bridgid's Day be fair and bright,
> Winter will have another flight.
> If St. Bridgid's Day be cold and rain,
> Winter's behind us once again.

St. Bridgid's Day (1st February), is the first day of spring and the beginning of the farming year. Every year many Northsiders made a St. Bridgid's cross from rushes, which was placed on the wall by the front door to keep mischievous little folk out of the house, and it was generally believed to bring good luck for the year.

Light and Water

'Throw all your candles and candlesticks away and go to bed with the light of day'. The long winter nights slowly got shorter as the day's light got longer. The moon was an important light source and when there was a full moon it was said that the 'parish lantern' was burning well that night. On Candlemas Day (2nd February) you took your tallow candles to the church to be blessed by the priest. In the past tallow candles were only used on Holy Days, but now-a-days beeswax candles are affordable.

The phases of the moon brought into the home

Way back, train-oil pressed from fish and fat from meat were used as light fuels. Then came the paraffin lamp and, later still, the tilly lamp, which gave a great light, and in the nineteen-sixties, two houses had a gas light fed from a cylinder. Mickeen Pairca (Michael O'Driscoll of the Poundland) didn't need candles as he went to bed with the dark and was up with the light throughout the year and so he had a good rest in the winter! A big change to the Northside happened on the 16th August 1977, with the switching on of 'the electric'. Everyone decided to have it. Most houses had a strip light and a socket put into the kitchen. The younger generation had great fun with the electric.

If the clouds were low, the rotating beam of light from the Fastnet would bounce over to the Northside

One older gentleman, who's name we won't say, had an electric kettle full of water on the kitchen table for over a year, while still boiling the old kettle on the open fire! The lads eventually took pity and showed him how to use it and he never looked back. Mind you, he took his time and would fill the electric kettle with water, a cup at a time, to the number of cups that he wanted, plus a half cup for luck, for the tea. It was an expensive business boiling the kettle with the electric! Perhaps it was a sign of how careful one had to be with money in times gone by.

Today, if there is a power cut, everyone runs about like scalded cats - can't do this, can't do that, can't do the milking and my goodness gracious me, what about the food in the freezer? Twenty years ago there wasn't that worry, but then there were others! Television took a bit of time to work it's way into the old houses but it helps to pass the long winter nights. The older generations' customs are barely remembered or are part of the way of life any longer. Now there is less scoriachting and you can do all your talking over the telephone, which arrived on the Northside in 1987. With the coming of computers, there's little need to move at all. You can now see and hear a person 'live' and have a chat using the computer whilst sitting in a soft, comfy armchair, with your feet up by the open fire. So what's next - a 'virtual' blast from the south-west to freshen you up a bit?

The water for home use came from wells and was drawn into the house first thing in the morning for the breakfast tea. Two houses often shared a well but it was said that you should never interfere with anyone else's well. All the Northside last used the Bone (everlasting) well at Canty's Cove in 1940, when all the others dried up in a drought. With the coming of the electric people piped water into the houses and it was a great hand for the women, but water is still drawn, by some, from their well for the tea and drinking. Tobernasool was a 'Holy Well' in Dunmanus West and if you had a wisp (watering of the eye) or a creabhour (a stye) you would wash your eyes three times with the water to get the cure.

The Start of the Farming Year

Most of the farms were small and had scattered fields, with plenty of rocky patches, which made hard work. Only a few farms had land of adjoining fields.

It was said that Danny O'Donovan got his large piece of land, that was not broken up, from the landlord (the Earl of Bandon) when he visited Dunkelly. Lord Bandon was just about to jump down from his horse drawn car, when Danny took off his cap and threw it down on the earth. He then cupped his hands to allow his lordship to step down in a more leisurely style and as he did so, Danny said, "Good morning my Lord, put your foot in that, and how's the Lady Mary?" That was good enough for the Earl of Bandon and he enquired of Mr Donovan as to what he would like in the way of land. Danny said that he was after a piece of ground that was in one piece, so that he would not have interference from any other man. His wish was granted!

There were two other men to have their land in one piece and they were Johnny Mosseen (John Downey) at Gurthdove, and Roycroft in Dunkelly East. Mosseen had one gneeve, said to be the grass of four cows (or half a ploughland). The 'gentleman' farmer, Roycroft, wore white gloves and a starched white collar when farming and he didn't last long on the Northside. He sold his thirty-five acres in Dunkelly East, to Jeremiah Scully from Goleen who made a great hand of it!

The sheep's cró on Knocnaphuca

The rougher hillsides and bogs were open commonage, shared by the farmers for grazing cattle and sheep and digging turf for the fire. There were a few crós (animal shelters) for sheltering animals on the commonage. One cró, on Knocnaphuca, is built at a béillic (cavern at the base of vertical rock face) and has a curved dry stone wall with one end open and a stone slab roof.

Slab stone roof of the sheep's cró

Other cró were for donkeys and at Gurthdove there is a bull's cró that was used for hiding the bull from the authorities, so as to save on the licence.

The Ridge of Graf

In the first week of February you would begin on 'the Ridge of Graf' (lazy bed system) using a dry, sunny and sloping ground to give an early crop of potatoes. The 'Ridge of Graf' system, although hard work, would give you up to three times more crop than setting potato seed in a drill. A good supply of manure was used and you would use stable manure (horse or

Potato ridges unused since the Great Hunger

The grafán, gabhlóg, hook and potato spade

donkey) as it was said it had a better 'heat to it' than yard (cow) manure. The stable manure was spread on to the grass and the seed potato placed on top. This was then covered with the sods, cut with a grafán to open a trench on each side, of 18-20 inches. This gave you a ridge of about three feet. Soil from the trench was then put up on the ridge. This was called 'the first earth'. The last shovel of earth from the trench was put against the edge of the ridge, and with a good pat from the back of the shovel, the grua (side of ridge) was made.

One man was hacking ground for a farmer when he was called in for morning tea. Before going in, the farmer said "That's tough old pucking there, I suppose?" To which your man said, "It was." The farmer replied with a great show of ingratitude, "You're tough enough for it." With that your man stuck the grafán in the ground, leapt over the ditch, and away with him he went!

The 'Field bán' (crop rotation system)

To plough a 'field bán' was to use the old crop rotation system. In the first year you would set the main potato crop, the second year corn or wheat and in the third and fourth year the field would be left as meadow for hay. In the fifth year the field was used for animal grazing. After the grazing you would go back to setting potatoes the next year. You should not sow or set any crops on St. Gobnait's Day (18th February), as this would bring you bad luck. If a man was passing by and he met someone working in a field, he would start the conversation with "God bless this work".

Work would start on the main crop of potatoes by late February and the seeds would be set in ridges at the latest by St. Patrick's Day to be ready for the table by August. In the past seed potatoes were used but later sprouters were preferred. The seed potato was a whole potato with all but two eyes scraped away with a knife. The sprouter was a slice of potato with two good sprouts. If you had pieces of potato left over from cutting the sprouters they were called the scalabóg and were boiled and fed to the pig or hens. After spreading the manure or seaweed from the cart, you would plough the field into ridges of four or five scrapes, and then hack the ridge with the grafán and comb in the grua to make the ridge totally straight.

Jerry Paty, digging out sand, 1979

Three seeds or sprouters would be set in a row across the ridge. For the seed potato you dug in the potato spade as deep as the bucán (foot rest), then took a seed from the pouch and dropped it in. For sprouters, one man made the hole and another man placed the sprouter into the hole. Both types of seed were covered with earth using a farraheen (tool) to fill in the holes.

It was also time to prepare the ground for corn and wheat. There was a saying: 'Plough it deep while the sluggard sleeps and you'll have corn to sell and keep.' After ploughing out the tillage, yard and stable manure, as well as sand and seaweed, were spread on the land to improve crops. Different points along the shoreline had names so that every land user wanting seaweed had his own marked area. The seaweed was cut on the deep tides (spring tides), at the times of the dark moon (new), with a hook attached to a long pole.

> Once, when out cutting weed, a man was standing rowing in the stem (bow) of the boat when his dowel (rowlock) cracked and he went overboard. His singlet (vest) became caught on the iron keel band of the boat. It was lucky that he was an able and strong swimmer and that his singlet was worn and threadbare, for it gave way and he was able to surface.

> A man was setting his potatoes and using seaweed fertiliser. He did not get enough seaweed on Saturday and he knew that he would not have the tide his way on Monday. So after Mass on Sunday he harvested and spread the seaweed and said that if he had a sin committed God wouldn't let a bit grow. And so it was, as nothing grew on the ridges ever after.

Sand used for fertilising the fields was collected by Northsiders from Coosnastaighre (Cove of the Stairs) and later in the nineteen-thirties from Barley Cove, on account of the grant from the County Cork Committee of Agriculture. The further you had to go the more you were paid for your travel. It was a good way to get money into the country areas. In the nineteen-thirties the grant was 10/- a cart load from Barley Cove to the Northside. Rick Allan (Richard Collins of Dunkelly West) was buried up to his neck in sand one time, when an overhang in the sand banks at Barley Cove gave way. The man was all right but well shaken by the event.

Lambs, Bonhams and Baskets

Lambing took place from St. Bridgid's Day to St. Patrick's Day and it was a time of sleepless nights as well as a time to watch out for raiding foxes. Bonhams (piglets) were born in February and August and for six weeks would be kept under the stairs. Often, the bonhams would sit up close to the open fire and when the fire sparked, out they started, leaping and squealing. If going home late at night and you saw a light in a house, you would say that they were up minding the bonhams.

Furze (gorse) had many uses around the farm. It was found in plenty on rough, rocky ground in fields called 'breaks' as well as on hillside commonage. As a fodder, for cattle and horses, the new growth of small Irish Furze, was cut using a bill hook and gabhlóg (a stick with a 'V' at the end) but if the winter was hard and fodder in short supply, the bigger French Furze was cut as well. The furze was then mashed with a mallet to soften it before feeding it to a beast. Since the turn of the century girls used a furze cutting machine to cut furze for horse feed. There were big, sharp blades that rotated very quickly when you turned a handle. If you weren't careful when feeding furze into the machine, a blade could take the top off a finger, and this in turn would mean that she was

A basket of barrfhód for the fire

unable to milk cows dry and so would be unacceptable to a farmer in marriage. The French Furze was also used for blocking gaps in ditches and as fire wood, and Irish Furze for animal bedding and guttery (muddy) areas in the haggard.

When the weather was too bad to step outside, baskets were made from twigs and rods (different species of coppiced willow) that had been cut on November Dark (New Moon). Wild rods and twigs were used for basket work such as back-loaders (creels) that sat on a wooden straddle supported with straw mats for donkeys backs, sciffs for the table potatoes, cisean baskets for turf and potatoes, bird baskets and lobster pots.

A pair of donkey back-loaders (creels) for turf and potatoes

Ship wrecks

There have been many ship wrecks between Brow Head, The Mizen and Three Castles Head, and along Dunmanus Bay to Carbery Island. The main season for wrecks was between October and April. South of James's Sleabh, at Gurthdove, the Field of the Man was where drowned sailors were buried on the Northside. There is a large, rounded rock that marks the site of the communal grave. The last unknown sailor to be taken from the sea was in the nineteen-twenties. Ned Hodnett made a coffin from boards taken from the loft floor of his cow-house. He had to make holes in the bottom of the coffin to let the sea water out when they raised the decomposing sailor from the sea.

The 'Iberian' was en route from Boston to Liverpool when she met thick fog and lost her bearings. She ran aground near Bird Island on 21st November 1885. She had a cargo of cattle and a crew of 54 all of whom survived. The 'Iberian' broke up in a storm on 15th October 1886.

On a hardy November night in 1885, some sailors came knocking at the door of the Hodnetts in Gurthdove. They looked badly shook and they explained that their ship, the 'Iberian', was wrecked up the shore a bit. One of the sailors was kind of mad so they tied him down onto the settle, and after a time he settled down. The 'Iberian' went aground at Carrigahomes just south-west of Bird Island. Two of the sailors headed for Crookhaven to telegram for steam tugs. There was cattle, flour and general cargo on board her as well as leather that was good for making boots at the cobblers. Some flour stacks were collected, the wind changed direction and the rest were swept away. A long time later they returned, by which time the salt water had hardened some inches of the flour in the sacks giving a shell to the loose flour inside. A good few sacks were collected on the second time around, and what flour wasn't wanted for the house met a good market at High Street Schull.

The 'Memphis', built in 1890, was a 3191 ton and 345 foot ship of the African SS Co. She was en route from Montreal to Avonmouth with bacon, butter, cattle, flour, lead ingots, timber and other general cargo, when she was wrecked at Dunlough Bay on the 17th November 1896. Nine of the crew were drowned but many other lives were saved by local people.

All the able seamen from the Northside went up to Dunlough, near Three Castles Head, to the wreck of the 'Memphis'. There was one old fellow left at home, he was Johnny Hodnett of Gurthdove. In his time, he had been a great man on the water and he was mad to go to the wreck. Johnny couldn't get any seasoned men for a crew as they had all gone to the wreck. The situation was picking at him and after a spell he pulled out a handful of young fellows that didn't know much about the sea at all. He set off with himself at the tiller and with the lads pulling as hard as they could. They arrived at the wreck and Johnny masterminded a route through the other boats. There was great scratching, scraping and screeching but they kept all the other boats at bay. They were the first to have their boat fully loaded with bacon, butter, flour and timber. They pulled out and were the first home, and your man with a new-seasoned crew!

The 'Oswestry', built in 1888, was a 2419 ton 300 foot steamer. She was en route from Newport News and Norfolk Virginia to Manchester when she met heavy fog and on the 12th March 1899 was wrecked at Mizen Head. With thanks to locals the Captain and crew all survived. There was a cargo of cotton, deal, copper ingots, iron plates and Indian corn.

Men from Gurthdove and Lackavawn decided to go by boat to see if there was any wrack (flotsam) to be had from the 'Oswestry'. She had a cargo of, amongst other things, copper ore. The men took Johnny Murphy with them as he was kind of wild and they knew that he'd board her. They put your man on the ship and he went down into the hold and got a bar of copper. Johnny came back up onto deck. He shouted down to the seine boat that he was letting the bar down by rope, but he hadn't put the right kind of hitch on the copper bar and it slipped before he had the words out. The bar went down between two ribs and opened a plank in the waiting boat. There was an almighty flood of water. They quickly put a jacket into the hole to stem the flood. The angry men talked for some time about whether they should leave Murphy where he was, on the 'Oswestry', or to take him back with them! They had to shore up the boat at Dunlough and as they walked home they asked Wild John Murphy why didn't he give them good warning as to when he was going to let the bar down. "Blast you," he said, "I told you when I was leaving it down!" The bars sold for 3/- each to the customs men but a better price of 5/- to other buyers.

The 'Oswestry' at Mizen Head, 12th March 1899

The 'Lusitania' was sunk on the 7th May 1915 with the loss of 1,200 lives. The windows shook in Goleen school with the blast of the torpedoes.

The last really bad storm was in 1952 when there was the devil of a gale. The sea was swept 'mountains high' and went over Carbery Island, up over the road by Cuasgorm and out east for Reen. It had all the place carried, even the ditches at Tadg's and James's Sleabh. Now that was some power!

The Wreck of the Iberian

Come all you gallant heroes that dwell around Erin's shore,
And likewise pay attention to these few lines composed.
It's of a jolly steamship, from Columbus she set sail
To cross the Atlantic Ocean, the Iberian by name.

When we left the port of Boston our captain he did say
"We'll have a speedy passage across the raging main."
The fog it proved deceitful along our native shore,
Which purplexed our navigator in the róws of Carrighomes.

When the crew had landed to Crookhaven they made their way,
They telegraphed for tug steam boats to come without delay
To take her from our ancient isle to Liverpool in tow,
But the Atlantic's foaming water approved their overthrow.

The tugs arrived next morning just at the break of day,
With gloomy hills and mountains and headlands in the bay,
Then to their astonishment her poops were overthrown
With her ropes and mast and rigging in the róws of Cuasnagno.

Thank God there is great plenty now along our native shore
From Brow Head Point to Sweet Cape Clear and along to Baltimore.
All the small boats in the harbour are paddling through the bay
And they are loaded to the waters edge, and homewards with their prey.

Long life to the noble captain though we can't tell his name,
That he may be highly rewarded with honour and great fame,
With his pockets full of silver, likewise of solid gold,
And the blessing of the people be with him wherever he may go.

The Memphis

When the Memphis she did leave Montreal, the weather they said was fine,
Said the captain to his officers, we'll have a pleasant time,
But before she reached the Irish coast, there came a heavy fog,
The captain lost his reckoning, by an error in his log.

On the 17th of November at eight o'clock at night,
The lookout man at Forecastle Head, thought he saw a light,
He took it for the Fastnet Rock, and sorry I am to say
That 'twas by that fatal error, she was wrecked at Dunlough bay.

When the Memphis struck the rock that night, our captain he did say,
"Brave boys, she'll go to pieces, and we'll be cast away,
So lower down the lifeboats, and try your life to save,
I trust in God that none of us will meet a watery grave."

We lowered our starboard lifeboat and she was fully manned,
But before she reached the waterline the aft-tackle jammed,
The forward one went on and the boat she swung around,
The crew got in the water and nine of them were drowned.

We lowered our port lifeboat and the painter was made fast,
The crew was getting into her, the captain was the last,
But a mighty sea came rolling in to sweep the boat away
And left our captain to his fate, that night in Dunlough Bay.

The captain being a brave young man, with courage stout and brave,
He sprang up from the rigging his precious life to save,
But before he could do so another sea came on
And swept our captain over board, we thought his end had come,

The captain of the Memphis there was luck for him in store,
He got upon a bullock's back and safely got ashore,
Where he was kindly treated by the people there next day,
And that concludes my little song of that night in Dunlough Bay.

March

Mikey Hodnett with pollock at Gurthdove Pier

March was a month of many weathers and the days became long enough to tire a man and his horse. The corn and wheat were sown. Shrove Tuesday was a day for matchmaking before the strictly observed fasting and Masses of Lent began. Fishing from the rocks started on St. Patrick's Day followed by a Kitchen Dance.

A match made in c. 1860. Photograph c. 1900

Lent

Lent would be upon you during February or March and there would be plenty of fasting and Mass. Shrove Tuesday was the eve of Lent and it was traditionally the day for matchmaking. At the beginning of Lent, Ash Wednesday was a fast day, when black tea and dry bread only were eaten. 'Fasting and prayer is good for a sinner but a working man needs his dinner'. The hearth slat would gather ash and embers but none left the house that day. The first of the year's spring Stations were held from the Monday after Ash Wednesday. A brief break from Lent was on St. Patrick's Day.

Matchmaking

'To know a person right you'd have to eat a hundred weight of salt with them.' Nonetheless, Shrove Tuesday was a day for Matchmaking. It would set you up for what was to come! A bottle of whiskey was carried to the house where the match was to be made with the father of the girl to be wed. If an agreement was reached the hob was struck and the match maker would say, "Would you let this girl be buried with this man's family?" At this point the usual reply was "I will." Wild Johnny Murphy, (who got his name when one day he leapt the church gate in anger when a Priest

A marriage stone at Dunkelly West

asked him why he hadn't taken the sacraments), and Maggie Coughlan were both match makers on the Northside. Although it was said that a marriage made by a priest or woman would never work, Maggie changed all that!

Marriage stones were stones with holes carved through them. After a match had been made the couple held hands through the hole, to bring the marriage luck. This custom was still in use up to the nineteen-twenties.

Tuesdays, Thursdays and Saturdays were the days on which to get married. If two people from the same family married in the same year it would surely bring bad luck. The breakfast was held at the bride's home but later would move to the 'drag' home, where the bride and groom were going to live. If a Budarí from across the bay (we have no intention of directly translating Budarí; it's enough to say that it reflected on the virility of the men of Kilcrohane) was to steal a Northside girl it was bad luck, but on the other hand it was a good omen and a day to remember for a Northsider to steal a girl from Kilcrohane!

The Matchmakers and the Butter

There was a mother and daughter living on the Northside. The mother said that it was time to be making a bit of butter as it was coming up to Shrove Tuesday and that they could have matchmakers.

They put the cream into the churn but if they had stayed at it for a year and a day it wouldn't have made butter. The mother said to the daughter that they should put the cream into a ceiler and that she would jig a tune and that the daughter should dance in it. Before long they had a good lump of butter made. It was put up onto the corner of the table and the mother turned to the daughter and began to wash down her legs. The dog came from under the settle and yapped down the butter and away with him he went, out of the door. After drying her daughter's legs the old woman turned around to where the butter should have been. The mother gave a great roar and asked her daughter had she seen anything? The daughter replied that she had seen the dog go out the door with something, alright.

The mother called in the dog and said to the daughter to catch the dog by the ears and that she would work him by the tail. They rose him up as high as they could and let him drop down. After the third drive the dog threw up the butter, out onto the floor! The mother picked it up and then shaped it.

With the arrival of Shrove Tuesday the matchmakers came and a deal was met and the hob was struck. A fine tea was set before the matchmakers and when it ended up they said that it was the finest butter that they had ever tasted. Today we are all talking about pasteurising but that was all that the butter got that day!

The couple had children in basketfuls, lived long and died happy.

The Pride of Carbery

I am a youthful lover that has toured this world o'er,
To change my life and get a wife, I came to Erin's shore.
I visited Killarney's Lakes where beauty there it smiles,
Then I did stray along the bays to Carbery's Hundred Isles.

I wandered down those fairy dells from the summit of a fairy mound,
I hired a boat and jumped afloat, out from the Holy Ground
I skipped up through that island with a heart so light and free,
It was there I spied my Molly dear, the pride of Carbery.

Her cheeks were like the lilly, her eyes were as black as sloes,
The line of the equator was no straighter than was her nose
I asked her where she did reside, "Dunmanus, Sir," said she,
I then embraced my Molly dear, the pride of Carbery.

I whispered love into her ear and then I did propose,
"Look at Dunmanus Castle dear, where dwelt the Macs and O's,
I will build it up in splendour, and forever more we will rest,
In it's lofty walls and lonely halls, where the raven builds her nest."

"Kind Sir, do not be too forward, for I am engaged before,
Look at that strand with its shells and sand, and the seagulls soaring o'er
It is there that dwells a fishermen, whom I ne'er can forsake
Who goes out each night with a heart so light, to fish for cod and hake."

"Oh Molly dearest Molly, you know it is not fair,
To have you wed a fisherman and I a millionaire,
With your gentle fairy figure, in your humble skirt and shawl
I would build for you a castle dear, as high as the China wall."

"Kind Sir, look at those farms all with their horses and their kine,
Now if you were to own them all, and then that you would be mine,
To have the gold of San Francisco, kind sir it would be in vain,
I would rather marry Jimmy, with the faller and his seine."

Now all you youthful lovers who have toured this world all around,
Beware of the Dunmanus maids and the dolls of the Holy Ground.
Or if you don't I hope you won't be mesmerised like me,
By charming, lovely Molly, the pride of Carbery.

And now that I must say goodbye, though sad to me it seems,
For I must go and face the foe at the siege of Mons and Rheims,
For the beauty of Dunmanus it was too much for me,
Likewise charming, lovely Molly, the pride of Carbery.

Meallán showing the natural arch - 'Hole Open'

Stabbing the Cuiltán

St. Patrick's Day (17th March) was the day of 'The Stabbing of the Cuiltán'. It was the custom on the Northside to go to the South Point on Meallán to catch a small fish called the Cuiltán (Montegue's Blenny). This was done at low water using a pole with a beard (barb) on the end of it. The fish were found in scuttles (cracks) of rock at the shoreline. Many happy hours were spent by all before enough fish were stabbed to fill a half-gallon container. The cuiltáns were boiled on the open fire and eaten whole.

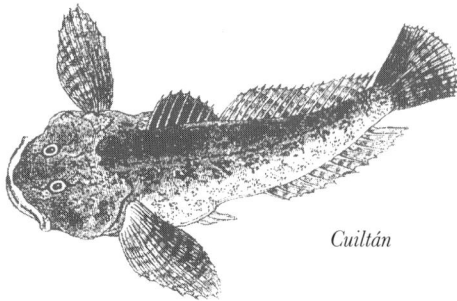

Cuiltán

'The connor hit his head on the rocks on St. Patrick's Day'. This is also the day when you started to catch the connor (wrasse) off the rocks. At certain places along the shore where the connor bites, you can find prash holes and stones. These are found at:

> Timmy's Mooring, Cuasacopóg, Spar Rock, Gardeneen, Speirhumber, Pollamúislee, the wall at Gurthdove pier, Slate Quarry, Béillic of Meallán, Point of Meallán, Eirn Garbh, Slios, Liceens and Cioun. Towards Bird Island; Gola, Red River, Brandy West, Brandy East and Liceens by Island.

Prash holes and stones were used to grind mussels and limpet, which were then scattered along the shore, as a ground bait, to attract the connor and pollock. This was called prashing and was done the day before you worked the rod, and on the day itself. The rod was a long wooden pole of twelve to fourteen feet and a line of about the same length with a mussel on the hook. When you got a bite, you had to strike quickly or the connor would fasten itself on weed or in a scuttle. You can also catch good size pollock at the same points along the shore. Fresh connor is sweeter to eat than mackerel or pollock and corned (pickled) connor was thought of as better for lobster pot bait than any other fish. West at Slios, James Coughlan (Lackavawn) and Jerry Paty were fishing for connor when James hooked one but it made fast to the weed and it wouldn't give in. " A deal mishá," cried James, "the sucker will give in after a while!" He wedged his rod and they set off away home for some grub. When they returned to the rocks they found the connor floating, dead from determination!

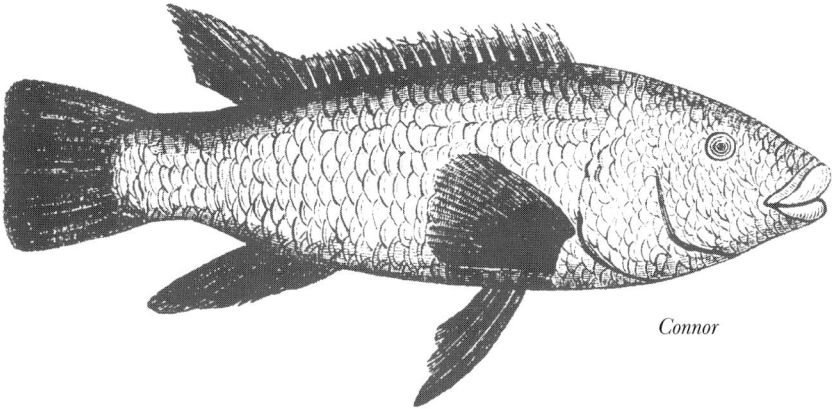

Connor

Pollock

William Downey

It was in the year of 1905 that William Downey, one of two sons and a daughter of a widow woman in Gurthdove, went down to Spierhumber, near Gurthdove pier, to fish for connor. He said to his mother to keep the dinner and that he would bring the cows with him for milking when he came home.

Early the next morning, when the men (Jack Collins and others) returned from seining, they saw William on the hill and said that his donkey must have been after breaking out again and that he must be looking for it. They were shocked and amazed when they were told that he had been drowned the evening before. The sea and shore was searched by all the men and there were plenty of men and boats in those times. The seine nets were shot but they got nothing. Everyone was out searching and still the body hadn't been found.

The Curate priest of Goleen, Father Desmond, who was on a sick call in the townland, heard the story of William Downey and that his mother was crying and lamenting to have her son's body found, and that only then would she be satisfied.

The Priest asked to be taken to the woman and he told her that she would have him returned, dead or alive, before night. The priest went to the Gurthdove Cuas, put on his stole and said some few prayers, Father Desmond then picked up a stone and said, "Wherever this stone lands, there will William Downey lie." Father Desmond threw the stone and it went only to the shore. He picked up another, it landed near the stern of a boat. The Priest said to the man in the stern to look out. Sure, didn't William's body slowly come up to the surface, head first, which showed it was death by accident, in the very spot that the pebble was thrown.

Father Desmond waited until William was in the boat. He went to the mother and said, "Now you have your son, but he is dead." William Downey was carried back to Gurthdove, waked and given a decent burial. He lies in Kilmoe cemetery.

Out of Firing

There were near enough no trees on the Northside and firing (fuel for the fire) was never too plentiful. Turf (peat) and Barrfhód (top sods) from the hillsides were the main firing, but borháns (cow pats), and donkey droppings that had dried out the summer before and stored were also used. By March, in a hard winter, you often would be running out of firing. Furze, stem and root, gave a great heat, also fern would be pulled and dried before using, but het (heather) could be put on the fire straight a way.

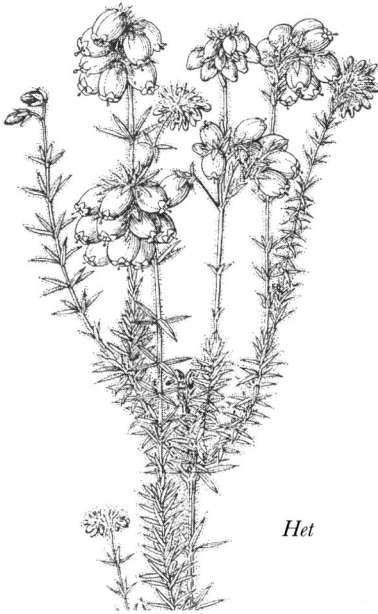

Het

Women would go to Dhurode Beag to gather a bundle of het which was pulled root and all. One woman pulled up a bush of het and she noticed a croc (round pot) of gold under it, in the ground. She let the bush back down and took off her garter and put it around the het, and then moved away to where the other women were. She filled her bundle and went away home with the other women. Before nightfall she went back to Dhurode for the croc of gold. To her surprise there was a garter around every bush of het! She said that it was more than good enough for her and that if she had shared what was in the croc, there would have been enough for all and the fairies wouldn't have put it out of her sight.

Sowing the corn

Sow corn in the gutter you'll harvest it in the dust.
(Sow in the wet and you will harvest in the dry)

With the land prepared in February it was time to sow the corn. This was done either by hand or using a hand held machine called a 'fiddle' that would cast a measured amount of corn with a good evenness. Apart from feed for the animals, corn is used in the making of poteen and, at certain times, as during the two wars, you had to tell the authorities how much you were growing. Glad to say, this didn't always happen and there was some fine liquid produced in the area!

Kitchen Dances

On the night of St. Patrick's Day there was always a Kitchen Dance on the Northside and it lasted until the dawn of the next day. Kitchen Dances, also called 'balls' or 'kitchen parties', were big townland dances that were held on special days of the year in the colder seasons: St. Patrick's Day, November Dark (at the end of the seining season) and soon after the Wren Ball on St. Stephen's day. In the warm summer months, dances outside in the fresh air were called 'Patterns' and they were held on Holy Days or on Sundays. There was never any dancing in Lent except for St. Patrick's Day.

The Kitchen Dances cost two shillings and six pence, but the Wren Ball would cost more. The Patterns cost one shilling. Women always went free of charge to dances but every able man had to pay. A tierce of porter (16 gallons) was provided for the event. When James McCarthy (Jim Will of Dunkelly Middle) was a boy in the nineteen-tens, he and Agnes O'Donavan (of Dunkelly West) were taught to play the squeeze box (melodeon) by Sergeant McGuire, of Goleen. He was then the only person to own and play a squeeze box. In the times before the squeeze box the dances were played on a fiddle or hummed out vocally. Sergeant McGuire performed for all the Kitchen Dances, playing;

> The Kilmoe Set, The Step O'Cipeen, Highland Fling, Polly Glide, The Stack of Barley, The Hornpipes, The Siege of Ennis, The Gay Gordons, and other, jigs, reels and set dances.

With the opening of the Goleen Village Hall, in 1926, the Kitchen Dance was banned, but they carried on with them on the Northside regardless. Michael O'Donovan (Mike Danny), Patrick Hodnett, Denis McCarthy (Dinny Willum of the Poundland, Dunkelly West) also learnt to play the squeeze box; they would each give a spell at it. Bat Downey, who played the fiddle, would come over from the South Side. There were some grand balls on the South Side as well. The favourite locations on the Northside were Pad Danny's (Patrick O'Donavan of Dunkelly North) and at the Wills (McCarthy's of Dunkelly Middle). All who came to the ball shared the cost of porter and whiskey, and a tierce of porter was provided for the night. Women wore fine, white linen blouses which became black when they danced, from the men's hands, dirtied by pipe baccy!

Agnes O'Donovan at her fireside, 1969

A Kitchen Ball

To ꝼꞃnd a Bꞃꞙde

Long ago in the olden days of Ireland, there lived a mother and son. It came to the time of year for marrying. The mother said to her son, "Jack, it's about time you got married." He asked, "Where will I go?" To which his mother replied, "Across the land." Jack struck out. He came to a farmer's house. He went in to make a match, as there was a girl inside. Hanging down from a beam was a piece of bacon. The old woman of the house said that it would stay there and only when the first child was born would it fall down. "Oh," said Jack, "and what would you give the man who would get it down?" "Five guineas," she said. Jack took down the piece, collected the five guineas and struck out for the road again thinking that they were mad anyway.

Jack travelled on when he came to a house with three men up on top of the roof with ropes and three down on the ground with a cow. "What are you doing?" asked Jack "There's a bitteen of grass up there on the thatch and it would help to keep our cow living," replied the old man. "You'll kill it!" cried Jack, "What will you give the man that'll feed the cow the grass." "Seven guineas," replied the old man. "Get a hook for me,"

Jack said. He went up, cut all the grass and threw it down. "For sure you're the best man that came today," said the old man and gave Jack the seven guineas. Once again Jack struck out thinking that they were mad anyway.

He travelled on and for sure it wasn't long before he came to another house with three men on the roof. Inside there was a big, old, open country fire place with yet three more men with a big rope around a white horse. "Bad luck to you!" cried Jack, "What are you wanting to be doing that for?" The men replied, "The horse is skinned on its back so we are trying to get him up the chimney so as to cure him." "What would you give the man that would cure the horse without putting him up the chimney?" "Ten guineas," replied the old man of the house. "Grand," said Jack, "fetch me a bucket and shovel." They did, and Jack went up the

chimney and brought down a bucket full of soot. He turned the white horse black. "Now you're all right," said Jack. The old man gave him his ten guineas and once again Jack struck out, thinking that they must be mad anyway.

It was not long before he met a farmer with lots of young bonhams (piglets) that he was getting ready for market. "Now," said the farmer, "I'll be away for a week and I'll give you five guineas if you feed the

bonhams, but mind that you don't feed the old sows much." The farmer arrived back after the week. Jack had given the feed to the old sows whose bellies were full and the bonhams were half dead with the hunger. "Oh cripes!" exclaimed the farmer, "I must thank you for what you've done. Here's your five guineas." Once again Jack struck out, thinking that they must be mad anyway.

Jack, by now, had had enough so he thought he would head for home. It was a fine day when he spied a small thatched cabin by the side of a hill. He went in. There was a fire lit with an old woman beside it. "For our good Lord's sake, where have you come from?" asked the old lady. "I'm just after coming from Heaven this minute," replied Jack. "That's great," said the old woman, "have you seen my son Mickeen there?" "I did," he replied, "and he has sent me to say that he hasn't a shirt on his back, nor pants, baccy (tobacco) or ne'er a damn thing." "Here's four shirts, four trousers and a pound of baccy, will you take them to my Mickeen?" "I will," said Jack, "but they're heavy things and I see you have a horse out side, can I take it?" "My husband is away and it's the horse that he works with," replied the old lady. "No matter," said Jack, "I'll let him back down your way."
Jack took the horse and away he went. After a few hours he thought that

someone might be agin him. He put the horse, clothes and baccy into a nearby cró and lay across the road. There he was, staring up at the sky as if he was dead and didn't your man who owned the horse come along. He bent down and shook Jack, "What happened to you, you look dead?" After a time Jack replied, "Oh no, but I got the biggest fright in all my life. Sure, didn't I see a white horse go up into the clouds?" "Don't let that bother you, that's the man who's taking clothes and baccy up to my Mickeen." "Is that the way?" said Jack. He got up and proceeded to walk away. When the man was out of sight, Jack went back to pick up the horse, clothes and baccy.

Jack married the first girl that he went matchmaking with, they had children in basket fulls, lived long, died happy and were never short of a twist of baccy.

That's my story for you, and with the help of God, I'll have another for you tomorrow night, sitting by the open fire.

April

Patrick McCarthy (Patsy Paty), out and about on his donkey. 1971

As April passed by, the darkness of winter lightened into the new born growth of spring as green went to emerald. The cows were put out to grass, the milk would start to flow and butter making went into full swing. Lent concluded after Easter Mass with a good feed and a Kitchen Dance. By the end of the month the cuckoo arrived and heralded the coming of summer.

Holy Week

Good Friday was a day of no work and a fast day, but you could eat fish, bread and tea. A well known saying was 'only eat shell fish when the month has an 'R' in it' and this custom was observed on the Northside. Before prayers at the church, many people went to the Cockle Strand near Crookhaven to gather cockle shells. Low water was always at 12 o'clock and prayers at 3 o'clock. Other eating from the shore included limpets, mussels and three seaweeds. It was said that the seaweeds should not be boiled and eaten before 'three drinks (tides) of the March water' as there would be little value in them. The seaweeds were: miabhán [meidhbheán], found on the north Mizen shore, trupán [triopán], found mainly on the south Mizen shore and slocán [sleabhcán], found on north and south Mizen shores. The other seaweed that was eaten, usually at breakfast, was carraigín (carraigeen moss). It was collected on the big (low spring) tide and then placed onto corrugated iron sheets or sacking and left to be rained on. After the first wetting it needed to be dried out and if the night showed signs of rain or a dew it would be brought into a dry outhouse. Carraigín was boiled with water to make a jelly, and it was said to be good for the relief of pain and asthma.

Before the sun rose on Easter Sunday, many people would rise to 'see the sun dancing Easter Sunday morning in'. Early on in the morning all the lads from the townlands would go around in a big group, blowing a trumpet made from a cow horn. The women of the houses visited would give them

Going to Mass by jennet and cart. 1970

boiled hen's eggs to eat, sometimes coloured yellow, from boiling with furze petals or onion skins. After Easter Mass everyone went home for a quiet day of rest and a good feed after Lent. The night would bring a ball with much drink and dance.

Getting Out and About

Once the roads were developed the means of moving goods around veered towards the land more than the sea. Donkeys, jennets and horses were all used for travelling to Goleen and elsewhere, whether ridden bareback, pulling cars, side-cars or traps. By the beginning of this century the bicycle came into use, and it was worth saving up for as it didn't need feeding like the donkey. On the larger farms the carthorse and float were used for general work. In 1974, Jerome Scully (Dunkelly East) was the first person on the Northside to own a motorised mode of transport. He purchased a Ferguson 20

Mary McCarthy off to Goleen with her Raleigh

tractor which made his and many other people's lives much easier on the Northside. It heralded the change of a style of life.

Root crops

Preparing the ground, in mid April, for sowing turnips was called 'raisting' and it was much the same as for 'the ridge of graf' but the sods, when turned, did not meet in the middle, and the gap that was left was filled with yard manure and prash (small mussels scraped with a potato spade from the rocks and then chopped and pulped) to prevent on turnips gout and thready. Scribes were made across the ridge about one foot apart and then the turnip seed was sown. The earth was rolled down with pit-props taken from wrack. A good heavy earth would stop the grass growing up and help to keep the turnips clean. They were thinned out, once five leaves were showing. Rape and yellow turnips that had been sown in July of the previous year were ready to pull and feed to cattle.

If yard manure was not spread in February for the setting of the 'Ridge of Graf', then, when the potato stalks were 6 to 8 inches high,

Con Scully's horse and cart. 1968

Jerome Scully and the first tractor on the Northside. 1974

guano fertiliser was spread on the ridges before the casting of the second earth. It was always best to earth in the evening, as the stalks would close up. Cabbage plants were set on the grua of the ridge of potatoes

Mid April was time for the casting of the first earth for the 'Field Bán' (main crop) potatoes. Seaweed was placed on top as a fertiliser which was harvested and spread out on the ridge. It would have to dry and then get wet again with rain before the casting of the first earth, which was made with three scrapes of the plough along the ridge. The earth was then cast onto the ridge and the grua was made straight with the shovel.

> Two men were working away in Canty's Garden earthing potatoes. The man, whose garden it was, hit something hard as he was scraping up the earth from the trench. He looked down to see that he had taken the lid off a croc (pot) of gold. Your man quickly covered the croc with a flick of the shovel and patted down the trench as a mark of where it was. Both men worked away for the rest of the morning until the mid-day meal at the house. Afterwards the man whose garden it was, said to the other man that he would go and get his pipe for a smoke. The man of the garden walked back to the trench only to find that the whole trench had been patted well down and so his mark was lost. It was said that there was enough gold for the two even if he had shared it, but as he was greedy the little people put it out of his sight.

Cows, Milk and Butter

When the grass started to grow, you would put the cows out to grass. Morning and evening, before bringing in the cows for milking, a wholesome grass was cut. With a rope you made up a shoulder bundle, or a 'bundle large', to take to the cattle in the cow-house. The grass was fed to the cows in milk to help increase their yield.

With the cats gathering for the occasion, the cows were milked in the cow-house by hand into galvanised buckets and you settled yourself on a strong wooden cow-stool. When walking past someone milking you had to be careful as, with a well practised and deadly aim, you would get a jet of warm milk straight from the cow's udder, onto the face! The same thing happened to the cats, but they stuck the pressure out and licked the milk up with glee. If the cow was a kicker, its back legs were tied with a rope called a spancil. The milk for the house went into an enamelled basin and for butter making it went into the ceiler to settle.

Maggie Courcey churning the butter

Butter was made by leaving the milk to settle for two days in an earthenware ceiler, well covered or you would soon find a mouse floating in it with it's legs up! The cream from the top of the pan was skimmed off, using a saucer, and placed into an enamel bucket. The sour milk that was left was used in making cakes (soda bread), but a drop was always left in the pan so that the next milk would set. When enough cream had been saved it was churned and made into butter. People and calves would drink the left over Butter-milk. It was great on a hot day! Thunder storms made butter making impossible. If someone was to call when you were churning, they would have to take a turn at the handle to keep the luck with the churn. Salt was added to the

A butter book. 1947

butter for home use, but for trading at the local stores it was made without salt. The cool linhay on the north of the house was always the place for milk products, but in the heat of the summer cabbage leaves were wrapped around the butter to keep it from melting.

A gypsy woman called to the Downey's at Gurthdove, and asked for a helping of milk. The woman of the house said that she could offer all the milk that the gypsy woman wanted, but that she could not give any butter as she hadn't much of it. The gypsy said that it was hard to make butter when the cream was being stolen from her. The Downey lady said that none of her neighbours would ever take the luck of the butter from her. The gypsy woman said that none the less, that it was the case, and that she would prove it to her. The gypsy went out and picked a pink herb, root and all, from the driest part of the hill and then washed it and placed it into one of the milking pans with a stone on top to weigh it down. "Now," said the gypsy, "keep the herb in the pan for three settings." The woman of the house and the gypsy thanked each other and parted ways. On the third setting of the milk the Downey woman tried to make the butter and succeeded with twice as much butter than before. There was plenty of fine butter in the house ever after.

The first creamery in the parish of Kilmoe was the Aughadown Portable Creamery Co., it operated from 1946 to 1959. The lorry would stop at the Dunmanus Cross, Kealfadda Cross, Court House Cross and east below the Kilmoe burial ground. Sean Flynn, who lived at Coslows at Dunkelly West, was the first lorry driver for the portable creamery. In 1959, the creamery near Goleen was built by the Aughadown Creamery.

The milk churns on the northside were put onto milk stands and then collected by a local man and taken to the Goleen Creamery. Richard Swanton did this until April 1963, followed by Donal Goggin, Con Scully and then Jerome Scully. Every morning Jerome went on the rounds with his cob and car, and later his tractor, to collect the milk churns from the stands at the roadside. Jerome went from Dunkelly East to West, and then back to Dunkelly Cross and up over to the south side, collecting all the way. On the Northside, ten farmers had milk for the creamery, five were in too small a way to have any spare milk, and five were on the pension.

Rush hour at Goleen Creamery

After a cow had calved the hairs on her udder were singed off with a candle that had been blessed at Goleen Church on Candlemas Day. The first milk after calving was called the 'boistin'. It was thick and very yellow. Many people thought of the 'boistin' as a special tonic and would drink it as it was, or mix it with wheat to make a good ríobún. The thick yellow milk lasted for three milkings before going back to the usual milk. A cow that missed calving, for one year, was called a stripper, and a cow that missed calving for two years was called a fornog.

Stray animals have always been around on the Northside and in Dunkelly there was a pound (for holding animals) marked on the 1840's Survey map in the area still known as the Poundland. In the times when there were many people and lots of food crops all over, it must have been important to keep the animals under control. The pound was also for confiscating cattle if you were unable to pay the rent to the landlords, and you didn't get the beasts back until the rent was paid. In the nineteen-tens

Taking the milk to the creamery. Timothy O'Sullivan, c. 1960

The milk stand at Dunkelly West. Last used in 1973

Jim Will (James McCarthy) remembered the Pound was moved to the Enaughter Townland, just by the Goleen Road and, "You had to pay to get your animal out again!"

Animal Cures

The veterinary surgeon is a comparatively recent expense on the Northside. Below are some of the past, home-made remedies for the curing of animals. The warble fly, was one of the worst menaces for cattle as it didn't have a local cure. The fly laid its eggs in the legs of the cattle and then the maggot worked its way up to the backbone before leaving the beast. The fly problem was eradicated in the nineteen-sixties when the government provided a chemical wash that cured it.

Wild goats in the ruins of Wilkinson's Store

Some animal diseases and their local cures

Cattle

Crúibínach (cow hoofrot) - Bluestone and lard mixed and put onto the hoof, and then cover it with sacking.

Blast (mastitis) – The yard manure is surrounded by liquid called 'múnluch'; take some of it and splash the quarter of the udder affected.

Timber tongue - Use a pair of tongs to open the cows mouth, light some straw with soot from the chimney and make the cow inhale the smoke.

Worm tail – Split the tail six to seven inches up from the bone and to a length of two inches. Pack the wound with soot and salt and then bind with a rag.

Ring worm in cattle (and people) – Equal measures of boiled copóg (dock leaf) root, sulphur and lard, mix together to make an ointment.

Bound cow – Bring the cow into the house for the night. More recently treacle and cattle salts were fed to the cow in the outhouse.

Thorns in the nose – Soak a length of foxy rope (sisal string) in 'Jeyes Fluid' and twist up the nostril.

Pink eye, Scale in the eye – Cut the end off a goose quill and then fill with salt and blow into the eye.

If a cow took a large lump of turnip and had a blocked gullet, the Notters in Colleras had a machine that went down the mouth of the cow and would remove the turnip.

Red scour (new-born calves passing blood) – Heat a rusty iron to red hot and immediately strike the iron a few times over boiled milk so that the rust (oxidised iron) goes into the milk and then feed to the calf. Repeat until cured.

White scour (calves up to two months old) – Starve the animal of milk and then feed it boiled briar leaves or strong tea, using a cow horn. Repeat until cured.

If a cow was poorly and not feeling itself, it would get a good dose of furze. It was thought a great tonic for beasts. Furze was also fed to ponies or horses as it would get their wind going.

Horse, donkey and jennet

Hair loss in a donkey or jennet (through heavy sweating when ploughing) – Boil a plug of baccy in a gallon of water and place the liquid on the bald patches. (Does not work on bald-headed men!)

Skin sores – Pat soot from the hob onto the sore.

Pigs

To cure cramps that often came on when a pig was kept in a chamber for the final fattening. A dose had to be fetched from the chemist in Ballydehob. Pigs were always difficult to dose, until one old man said to cut the top off an old Sunday shoe and to work that on the pig's mouth and to pour the dose down the shoe. It worked fine.

Sheep

Bloat in sheep – Stab between the third and fourth rib with a sharp knife.

Lamb's arf – Bluestone and lard paste rubbed on the arf.

Sheep footrot – Place plenty of lime in the sheep's paths.

Always remove loose teeth in old sheep.

Fowl

Ticks on the eyes of goslings – plenty of butter spread around the eye.

The cuckoo comes in April,
She sings her song in May,
In June she changes tune,
And in July she flies away.

Paddy Collins and the Cuckoo

The children had two rhymes for the cuckoo, so welcome was its call:

The Cuckoo is a pretty bird, she sings as she flies,
She brings us good tidings and tells us no lies.
She sucks the birds eggs for to keep her voice clear,
The more she calls cuckoo, the more summer comes near.

Paddy Collins (known locally as Paddy Green) and the cuckoo arrived at the latter end of April for the summer months. Paddy Collins was a travelling man and he came to the Northside every year until 1985. It was grand to see Paddy on the road, it meant summer was around the next corner and he'd have all the news from other parts. He'd stay at Mickeen Pairca's or Florry Pad Flor's in the Poundland. He was strictly honest and fond of prayers. If Paddy was in the house and there was £100 on the table, he wouldn't touch it. On a wet day steam would come out of his clothes when he pulled up by the fire, but he wouldn't bother about that. He was a decent man who would do odd jobs around the haggard and he also made brushes out of wire and horsehair. There was another travelling man who used to be fed and taken into the house for the night. He wasn't quite right in the head and when it came to the time for him to sleep on the kitchen settle, he would go outside and beat out the tune, the 'Stack of Barley' with his hob nailed boots, on the flag-stones!

Rent, Rates and Tax

Finding the money to pay your dues was an ongoing problem. In the days of the Landlords there was always a great worry about the threat of eviction if you couldn't pay the rent. Since the famine times the neighbours all pulled together to avoid evictions, but, even then, a few took place on the Northside. Rates also had to be paid to the County Council and they hung over one's head like a black cloud as well.

With all the Collins and McCarthys it was handy, as the authorities would get confused with the situation, although they did not have much call to be around the Northside anyway. The taxman was rarely seen on account that times were not easy, and it was hard to get blood from a stone.

The first public record of communication with the taxman was when Patsy Paty (Patrick P. McCarthy of Gurthdove), received an official letter in the nineteen-fifties when he was working on the roads. "At first I couldn't make it out at all, at all, but, with the power of spectacles, I came to a better understanding." The sad conclusion was that 'Mr. Patrick P. McCarthy' had a bill to pay.

A rent receipt from the landlord

The Tax Song

The members of our Parliament and rulers of our land,
They're going to tax the nation to keep down the working man,
Go where you will by day or night, this country you go through,
The people cry, "I wonder what is this that they mean to do?"
So no wonder people grumble at the taxes more and more,
You've never seen such taxes in old Ireland before.

They're going to tax the farmer, the horses carts and ploughs,
They're going to tax the billy goats, the donkey, pigs and cows.
They're going to tax the mutton, they're going to tax the beef,
They're going to tax the old ones that haven't got good teeth,
So no wonder people grumble at the taxes more and more,
You've never seen such taxes in old Ireland before.

They will tax the ladies hair nets, their bows, veils and hats,
They're going to tax the mice, the mouse's traps and rats.
They will tax the lady's flour scones, their high heeled boots and stays,
And when the sun begins to shine they will tax the rabbits and hares,
So no wonder people grumble at the taxes more and more,
You've never seen such taxes in old Ireland before.

They're going to tax our bachelors as heavy as they can,
They will double-tax old maidens who turn forty-one.
They will tax the ground we walk on and the turf that keeps us warm,
They're going to tax our children a month before their born.
So no wonder people grumble at the taxes more and more,
You've never seen such taxes in old Ireland before.

They have taxed the glass of brandy, ale, whiskey and rum,
They'll tax the tea and sugar, the baccy, snuff and wine,
They're going to tax the fish that swim and all the birds that fly,
They will tax the very nails in our coffin when we die,
So no wonder people grumble at the taxes more and more,
You've never seen such taxes in old Ireland before.

They're going to tax the crutches, they will tax the wooden legs,
They're going to tax the bacon, bread, butter, cheese and eggs.
They're going to tax our pensioners as heavy as they can,
They will double tax the girls that are looking for a man,
So no wonder people grumble at the taxes more and more,
You've never seen such taxes in old Ireland before.

They will tax the ladies and their paint and brides that walk with men,
They're going to tax the ducks and geese, the turkey, cock and hen,
They're going to tax the tea spoons, the dishes, knives and forks,
And they'll play the very devil with the Germans and the Turks,
So no wonder people grumble at the taxes more and more,
You've never seen such taxes in old Ireland before.

They're going to tax the corn fields, the potato garden too,
They're going to tax the cabbage plant, the jackdaw and the crow.
They're going to tax the hobble skirts and table up some laws,
But the devil said he'll tax them when he will get them in his claws.
So no wonder people grumble at the taxes more and more,
You've never seen such taxes in old Ireland before.   *(c.1916)*

May

Goleen Main Street, looking north. c. 1910

With the strengthening sun the spring flowers blossomed. People went out and about to fairs and markets and the boats were launched onto a blue and vibrant Dunmanus Bay, to collect gull eggs and put sheep up onto Bird Island. May was the month of many enchantments, but it was the wise person who guarded against some of them.

May Day

On the eve of May Day the cowshed was locked to keep the little people from entering, otherwise they could make mischief with the milk. May Day (1st May) is the first day of summer. The day had plenty of power (magic) to it and it was a day for piseógs (charms) to ward off the evil spells and magic of ill-intentioned neighbours. As the sun rose its head for the day you would bring the May Flower (yellow iris) and other greenery into the house to celebrate the arrival of summer. Maidens would wash their faces in the early morning dew to keep themselves beautiful for the year. Water, to last the family for the day, was brought into the house from the well but if you met anyone you had to throw it away and start again. The water, in part, was used to wash out the milk buckets with extra care, and any other containers that had milk or butter in them, as it was believed that this would bring extra luck. Fire, ashes, water, milk, butter or salt could not be taken out of the house that day, as bad luck would surely follow.

Elder branches cut and pointed towards another man's cowshed would take the luck from the beasts inside. It was a wise precaution to place the mark of the cross on your cattle's forehead, using your right hand, and again, cross the cow shed door and the milk churn, with a spánach (burnt furze stem). This would protect you against any spells cast by your neighbours, that might take the luck from you. To cast 'bunce' water over your cows would protect them from spells. The water would need to come from where two streams met, and one of the streams would have to be a 'bunce' marker (a boundary between two townlands). To take the luck of the land from a neighbour, you would place two hen's eggs, at sun rise, under a ploughed scrape on his land.

Bird Island

Trips to Bird Island to gather cóbach (black headed gull or generally any gull) eggs and later to land sheep on the Island for grazing, started the year on the water. There were various boats on the Northside; the seine and faller boats were big, heavy boats mainly for seine fishing but the faller was sometimes used for lobster potting. Boats for general use and lobster potting were rarely less than twenty-one feet otherwise they could be a danger if the weather turned rough. Small

punts (boats under twenty-one feet) were used in settled weather, and very locally, for casual fishing and jobs close to the shore such as cutting seaweed.

In the early part of May, cóbach eggs, from the steep and craggy Bird Island were collected and then boiled and eaten. Boats over twenty-one feet were always used, and it was best to set out with the going tide as there would be less wind. To get onto Bird Island was tricky as there was often a good heave (swell) in the

Bird Island from Dhurode

water, and only the rocks to land on. The bloc (anchor) was thrown near the Stakes on the shore side. The boat was then eased back, north-east to the island. The stem rope was tied off at the ring and you jumped onto Bird Island from the stern with a rope, tied to the tarft (thwart). She was then tied off onto a spur of rock. Once on land you climbed up the scuttle (rock face crevice) to the green on top. Long iron stakes were driven into the ground, and sturdy ropes attached so that you could climb down the cliffs. On the first trip down, sacks were placed where the rope met a point of rock to stop it fraying. With the cóbach going mad, it was a tricky job, to pull yourself back up with a hand basket and your pockets full of eggs, and often you would end up in a sticky situation! Only eggs from a nest with one or two eggs were taken, as if there were three eggs it meant that the first laid egg would be developing and no good to eat, and so they were all thrown into the sea. When a cóbach found it's nest empty, it would lay more eggs and give a chance for a second visit to the island, but after that you had to give them peace. On leaving Bird Island the stern rope was taken off as you pulled on the stem rope. This gave you clear water between the boat and land.

It was the custom of the Kilcrohane men not to go to Mass if the cóbach egg gathering fell on a Sunday, as this would mean that they could get a full day at the eggs. One Sunday a Kilcrohane man was a good way down a rope, swaying about, when the man at the top of the cliff saw that the rope had frayed to the last twist on a sharp rock. They called down for the man to stop moving and explained the situation to him, and he carefully came back up to the green. After this the Kilcrohane men always went to Mass before going to Bird Island.

Gull eggs were also collected from Carbery Island where the róns (seals) were always to be found. It was a gentler sport with a good landing place and easy ground to walk on. The Shaggas small blue eggs were also collected by boat from the Lug of Dhurode and Spureen. The taste of the Shagga's egg was too strong and fishy for many, and it was only the few who would care for them.

Scairavin na gró (Scairavin na gCuach, Wind of the Cuckoo), a sharp wind and showers that arrived in the middle of May, would last for about a week or so. It was said that it was the last blast of the winter. With the first settled patch after the Scairavin na gró there was another trip to Bird Island, this time with sheep. It was said that there was only one cargo worse than sheep and that was a boat full of women! It was a great day for the young and fit lads, and at least three would have to go. Fifteen sheep were taken from Canty's Cove at Dunkelly or the Pigeon Holes (Cuasnacolúr), on the south side of Meallán. Getting off at the island was a different matter and you needed a still day, as to get up onto the island, even with a gentle heave, was anything but a joke without a landing place. Once you had a man up, a rope was used to haul up the sheep. In the passing of four months on Bird Island the sheep would be as fat as pigs and as wild as the sea around them. It was the very devil to get them off again. By the time you had a brehóg of sheep in the boat, you would be sweating buckets!

On the Farm

Digging the 'Ridge of Graf' potatoes started about the 20th May, and enough for the mid-day meal and animals were taken each day. It was the month to 'put up the second earth' on the main 'Field Bán' potatoes. If the corn was coming up with a yellow cast it would be 'bushed', using a large furze bush tied to a horse and weighed down with slats (long thin slabs) so as to cover any exposed roots with earth. Mangolds were sown in the same manner as turnips, but the seeds were soaked in water for a week and you used fresh yard manure and seaweed as fertiliser.

There were plenty of pests around the haggard and fields besides the children sliding down the ricks. Badgers would go rooting in the Ridge of Graf and the garden for worms, in the hive for honey or even in the fowl house for eggs. They were a big nuisance and the garda gave a reward if any were caught. The grey crow and magpie would pick an eye out of a living beast that had got stuck and was unable to move, and of course, there was our friend the red fox, who was forever worrying the hens, turkeys and ducks. The only cure for the pests was a slap for the children, fresh tar and smoky fires for the badger, a scarecrow for the birds and the dogs and a gun for the fox.

Lindberg

A grand event was nearly missed, when in May 1927, Captain Charles Lindberg was the first man to fly solo across the Atlantic from New York to Paris. On the morning of the 21st he flew over Dunkelly and a few people saw him. Jim McCarthy was in a field below his house and Pad

James McCarthy (Jim Will) of Dunkelly Middle, who had flown when in America

Donavan and Paty Leary were in a field west of Pointamór. They all saw a plane come from the north-west. It was flying very low, and the two men in the field saw something thrown out. Away the plane went, up, up, up and away to the east, over the Scullys. The men went to find the object, it was a note in a metal canister, and it said, 'I am Captain Lindberg.' Not knowing who he was, they threw it away into the ditch. After a week or two everyone in the world had heard of Captain Lindberg and so they went back to the field to find the note, as they thought it might be worth millions! They did not find it but some years later when two fields were being knocked into one the canister was found but the note had rotted away.

Nan O'Donovan selling a goose on Goleen fair day. c. 1920

Provisions and Fairs

Before there were any roads on the Northside the mode of transport was by boat and sea. The distance to pull by boat from Canty's Cove to Bantry or Baltimore was the same at about thirty miles but it was a lot safer to go around Sheep's Head than to go around the Mizen and across Roaring Water Bay. It would be a special event to go to Bantry, and only an important purchase at the fair or the mill would get you there. Even with the arrival of the coast road in the mid eighteen-hundreds Bantry remained the big town for the Northside people. Bantry Fair was held on the first Friday of every month. Northsiders had their own drinking and eating houses, likewise other townlands had different houses, and if you had business with a man from a different townland you would have a good idea where you might meet him.

From the mid to late eighteen-hundreds there was a fair in Goleen in January, March, May, July, September, October and December, with a market each Wednesday, that the women went to with butter, eggs, hens and geese. The bank clerks came from Schull and set up an office. By the late nineteen twenties a big fair was held on the first Tuesday of each month.

The May Fair at Goleen, was always one of the bigger fair days of the year, and it started at the break of day. It would raise the money people needed to pay the rates, and the rents to the landlords. It was when the main draught of cattle were sold for the year, there would be a radlóc of yearling cattle and old cows in a poor and 'staggering' condition. Pigs and sheep were also sold. The side walks would be covered with harness and tackle that the Whackers were selling. Other stalls sold bastables, china jugs,

Goleen Main Street, looking south. c. 1910

plates, cups and saucers. There was everything that you could ever ask for, and much of the fine ware can still be found on the Northside dressers today. The people, all buzzing around, would be hot with wheeling and dealing. Plenty of talk, argument and drink was the day's craic. The price asked for a beast was never the price settled upon, and it

could take the whole day before a deal was struck with a spit and the slap
of the hand. There was counter dealing, gossip, scandal and outright lies
given out when dealing, and with the big heave, it was a wise man that
only listened to himself!

> There was a farmer and a dealing man who was trying to buy a
> beast off of him. The dealer asked would the farmer take the ticket
> for the beast. They agreed, but as the dealer was handing over the
> ticket the wind took it out of his hand and up into the air. Once
> again the dealer asked would he take the ticket for the animal? The
> reply came that if there was any weight of money behind it that it
> would have been down long ago!

Criochán O'Shea was a man who sang ballads on fair days, and went
around collecting with his cap and selling penny song sheets. Paddy Piady

1920's traders bills – all paid!

worked a whip and could take a smoke (cigarette) out of your mouth with
it and he also had tricks with ladders and cart wheels which he balanced
on his chin. Towards the end of the day a taoscán (half sack) of meat was
purchased from the butchers; you could have pig and cow heads, pig

crúibíns (trotters), corned beef and any of the lesser meats in it. If you were of a peaceable nature, or you had brought the family to Goleen, it was best to go home early as you could expect a good fight towards the late evening. The lock-up for the drunk and unable bodies was on the road to the pier, behind the police barracks, that was burnt down in the times of the troubles (nineteen-twenties). Sometimes there was a good pile of men, but after a night's rest they were let out, as the fire would have left them! With the opening of the cattle mart at Skibbereen in 1958, on occasions, the Northsiders started to make their way east. The Bantry and Goleen fairs slowly lost ground and by the early nineteen-seventies had died out.

By the eighteen-sixties Goleen started to take over from Crookhaven as the main commercial centre of the area and began to expand from a place with two churches and a barracks, to a village with commerce and industry. By the nineteen-hundreds the Barnetts had a drapery and grocery store, Camier a coal merchant, James McCormack had a hotel (six rooms), Harringtons was the baker and later the Post Office and general store, O'Mahony the fish buyer and coal, grocer and provision merchant, Scully's a general merchant and shipping agent, O'Sullivan the boat builder and Jack Dan O'Sullivan the black smith. Sunday was always the big day of the week, everyone would go to Mass and afterwards to the stores for their provisions. Times were hard and the stores were checked out for the best prices, and the word quickly got around as to what to purchase, and from where! There was always time and money for a drink; all the bars would be thick with smoke and full to the brim.

Local Stores

Closer than Goleen were the local stores that provided everyday provisions such as tea, flour and tobacco.

For many generations the Connells of Fort View had a store at Coals Cross. Northsiders would sell cream and eggs to the Connell's, who made butter to sell at the big butter market at Bantry. After saving long and hard, you may have been able to buy a butter churn. It was easier to carry pounds of butter once a week than cream every day!

Wilkinson's Store in ruins. 1985

Until the late nineteen-thirties the Burchills had a small store in Lackavawn. There was also a store just beyond the Mareens in Enaughter owned by James Wilkinson, a general provider of provisions.

In 1916, Wilkinson, owner of the store at the end of the Mareens, was making a bit of a garden out of the pool, south of the store by the marked rock. Johnny Mosseen told him not to, as it was where the little people washed their faces. Wilkinson said that there was plenty of water on the other side of the road for them. Different people shopping at Wilkinson's Store heard the warning sound of barrels being rolled when there was not a barrel in sight! Wilkinson had not cleared much of the fairy pool before he died all of a sudden.

The Coughlans took over the store until the 1950's when it was left to the Cantys and the store closed. At that time Miss Long built the tin hut just north-east of the store where she set up shop. She sold everything you might want and you could order coal and sell her your butter and eggs. Often cash would not change hands, and a tally was kept of the produce you gave against the provisions that you took. A reckoning in cash was made at the end of the year, or sooner, if the difference was getting too big.

The Sheehans had a home and store in the hills at Kilbrown. From 1918 Jer Sheehan provided Lackavawn, Gurthdove and Dunkelly with food and farming supplies. Jer got his supplies from Bantry until 1926, but after that the provisions arrived by boat at Goleen. More recently the Sheehans also had an open truck which Paddy Sheehan, a good man for the people and now our TD for South West Cork, filled with everything that you could ever want. He called once a week to the Northside, on a Saturday. The Sheehans moved the shop to Goleen in 1975.

Tea packet. c. 1960

Plant lore and other cures for people

Plant lore

Plants always played an important part in daily life, and in health. It was said that the best time to pick herbs was on a Tuesday, Thursday and Saturday, near to the full moon. Below are some plants with their local names, along with their cures, dangers and uses.

Barnicy Ann -   (*Euphorbia hybernia,* Bainne cich na n-Éan, Irish spurge).
                         Place the milky white sap on warts to cure them.

Blessed Heather -   (Clubmoss).
                         Good luck charm.

Bog bean -   (*Menyanthes trifoliata*).
                         Drink water of boiled stems and leaves for jaundice, colds, fevers and tuberculosis.

Briars -   (*Rubus* spp.).
                         Drink blackberry juice for cough and diarrhea.

                         Water of boiled stems and leaves cures white scour in calves. Briars also used as binding for potato pits.

Broom -   (*Cytisus scoparius*).
                         Gives a good heat when burnt. Also used as a brush or broom for the house.

Buchrillán Bhuide -   (*Senecio jacobaea*, Ragwort).
                         Poisonous to cattle and will cause a cow in calf to abort.

Copóg -   (*Rumex* spp., Dock).
                         Rub the leaf of the copóg on the affected part to ease nettle stings.

                         Make a paste of the root of the copóg with equal amounts of sulphur and lard and apply to cure ring-worm.

Carrot -   Remove the core of a carrot, fill the hole with salt, and stand the carrot up. Then collect the juice that seeps through and place on warts.

Elderberry -   (*Sambucus* spp.).
                         Drink juice of boiled berries to clear up the yellow cast of jaundice in old people.

Fairy Thimble -   (*Digitalis purpurea*, Fox Glove).
Drink water of boiled roots for heart complaints.

Fern -   (*Pteridium aquilinum*, Bracken).
When dried, gives a high heat to the fire when baking. It was often used when turf was running out in the spring of the year. Also used for wrapping cured fish or bacon.

Fionnán -   (*Molinia caerulea*, Purple Moor Grass).
For making sugán rope for farming, fishing and chairs. It is also a good fire lighter.

Fiocadán-   (*Cirsium palustre*, Marsh or Black thistle).

Flax -   (*Linum spp.*). Making linen yarn.
Boil up the flax seed until it is thick and put onto boil.

Fox Clove -   (*Saxifraga spathularis*, St. Patrick's Cabbage).

Fuchsia -   (*Fuschsia magellanica*).
Used for field boundaries, fuel and the hay rick berth.

Furze -   (*Ulex europeaus*, French Furze or European Gorse).
Used for blocking gaps and fuel.

    (*Ulex gallii*, Irish Furze or Western Gorse).
Fuel, fodder and tonic, for animals and their bedding.

Gheasadán -   (*Cirsium vulgare*, White thistle).

Het -   (*Erica tetralix*, Heather, Fróech, Cross-leafed heath, *Erica cinerea*, Bell heather and *Calluna vulgaris*, Ling).

    Pulled in the winter for firing.
Used as a brush or broom for the house.

Holly -   (*Ilex aquifolium*).
Christmas and Wren Day decoration for the house.

Lousewort -   (*Pedicularis sylvatica*).
Place in cream as a charm against evil when making butter.

Miniheens -   (*Ammophila arenaria*, Muirneach, Marram grass).
The best thatching material.

Pennywort

French Furze

Irish Furze

Woodbine

St. Patrick's Cabbage

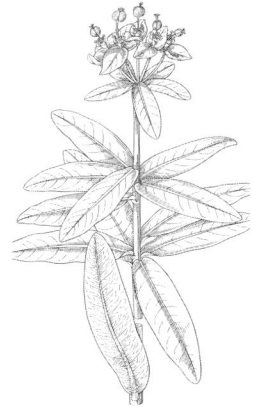

Irish Spurge

Mint -	(*Mentha* spp.). Make a tea with the leaves to help headaches and toothache.
Nettles -	(*Urtica dioica*). Boil the top leaves of nettles in May to eat as rich in iron.
Noinín -	(*Bellis perennis*, Daisy).
Pennywort -	(*Umbilicis rupestris*). Put the sap on bee stings.
Pipers -	(*Heracleum* spp., Hogweed). Used as a toy water pistol.
Reeds -	(*Typha latifolia*). Thatching.
Rib Leaf -	(*Plantago lanceolata*, Ribwort Plantain). Leaves placed on wounds prevents poisoning.
Rushes -	(*Juncus* spp.). Animal bedding, potato pits, St. Bridgid's Cross and baby rattles.
Sea Daisy -	(*Armeria maritima*, Thrift or Sea Pinks).
Sphagnum Moss -	(*Spagnum* spp.). Used as nappies for babies and in bandages to dress wounds.
Wild Garlic -	(*Allium* ssp.). Eat for stomach complaints.
Wild Sage -	(*unknown*) Drink leaves as a tea to strengthen brittle bones.
Woodbine -	(*Lonicera periclymenum*, Honeysuckle). Sweet smell for the house.
Yellow Iris -	(*Iris pseudacorus*, The May Flower). May Day decoration.

Trees

Elder -	(*Sambucus nigra*). To keep evil away. Traveling charm to keep the púcas away.

Elm -   (*Ulmus hollandica*, Dutch elm/ *Ulmus glabra*, Wych elm).
                       Boat construction and repairs.
                       Use a small branch to beat the caterpillars off cabbages.

Hazel -   (*Corylus avellana*).
                       Coppiced, and the 'rods' used for basketwork 'main
                       frame'. Traveling charm to keep the púcas away.

Twig -   (*Salix viminalis*, Osier willow).
                       Grown in the haggard. Coppiced, and used for
                       basketwork.

Wild Rod -   (*Salix caprea*, Goat Willow).
                       Found at pools and bogs. Coppiced, and used for
                       basketwork.

Non-plant cures for people

There was the doctor to go to but there were many local cures for
ailments. Mickeen Pairca was able to stop bleeding in people and make a
cows milk dry up using charms. One day William Downey cut his hand
badly with a hook, his life's blood was running out. So Mickeen Pairca was
sent for and he squeezed the wound together and said some few words
and the blood stopped pouring out. Mickeen told William to go and
bandage the wound up and that he would be fine, and he was.

Bad Joints -   Smear goose grease on the affected area.

                       The guts from crahogs (black pollock) were placed
                       into a container and left to rot down and the oil was
                       then rubbed on the areas of pain.

Beauty -   May Day dew was often collected into a bottle by
                       girls as it was said that using it on your face would
                       keep you looking young.

Bruises -   Goose grease or white bread boiled in a cup of
                       water and squeezed out and placed on the bruises.

Burns -   Plenty of cold water, preferably snow water, saved
                       in a bottle.

Corns -   Walk in the dew on the grass in the morning.

Cough, cold or flu -   A punch made from poteen with boiling water
                       and sugar.

Eye sores -	The water from a 'holy well' called Tobernasoul, was said to have the power to cure eye complaints.
	Fasting spit (your spit anytime before breakfast) rubbed into the affected eye.
Mental disorders -	See the priest.
Shingles (wild fire) -	Nick the right ear of a black cat and paint the blood around the infected area and say your name three times whilst doing so.
Tonics -	Bathing in the sea in the months of June and July is very good for you, as there is plenty of rotting seaweed (iodine) that is good for the skin.
	Some seaweeds, lightly boiled, and also nettles are good tonics.
Toothache -	Hold methylated spirits in your mouth for a minute or two and then spit out.
Warts -	Crush a snail between two rocks and place the juices of the snail on the wart and by the time the snail has decayed the wart will have gone.
	Three washes of the water from the ballaun (cupped rock) at the gate of Kilmoe Church was said to cure warts.

Ballaun Stone at Kilmoe Church

The Three Brothers

In olden days in Ireland, there lived three brothers. They all worked and lived on a farm. Two of the brothers worked well on the land. The other brother wasn't as handy for he used to go away every, and all day, hunting. He would not be back till late at night. He was of no use to them. Finally the two brothers decided to build him a cabin and give him a bitteen of land, two cows and his mother to look after, to see if that would get him to work. The brother worked away at the cows and land for about a week, when he heard the hunting horn, he was away. After four days he arrived back home to find his two cows dead.

The brothers came over and enquired as to what he was going to do. "I don't know," replied Jack, "I'll skin them later on and take the hides to town to make a bit of money." He did. Jack struck out along the road and after a short while he stopped for a rest. Didn't a magpie come along and start picking at the skins? He caught it and put it into the pocket of his coat. He carried on and after a spell he arrived at the town where the butcher was. He spoke to the butcher's wife, who said that himself was away for three days. "No harm," said Jack, "it wouldn't matter if it were a week." Jack knocked around town a bit. Sure, didn't he look through the window of the butcher's house only to see a man at the table and the butcher's wife putting a bottle of whiskey and a roasted turkey up into the press. That set Jack thinking.

The day came for Jack to see the butcher. In he went. The butcher gave him a sovereign for the skins as he had had a long wait. The butcher asked Jack if he would have a bite to eat; albeit not too grand, as they didn't have too much money. They went in and sat down. Jack leant against the magpie and it let out a screech.

"What have you there?" cried the butcher.
"Oh," said Jack, "that's a magpie I have in my pocket. It can tell me everything that happens whilst I'm away."
"What did he say now?" asked the butcher.
"The magpie says that there's a roast turkey up in the press!"
"No," said the butcher, "we can't afford that."
"I'm telling you," said Jack, "this bird tells no lies!"
The butcher went to the press and sure enough wasn't there a fine turkey there.

The wife was going mad, and they ate some of the bird. Jack knocked another screech out of the magpie.

"What's he say now?" asked the butcher.
"That your wife has hidden a man under the bed in the bedroom!"
"We'll get him out!" cried the butcher.
They did.
"Come away with me for a wetting in the bar," said the butcher. "You know I haven't so much money but I'd like that bird, it would be very useful to me. I'll give you two hundred sovereigns."
"No, no." said Jack.
They arrived at five hundred sovereigns and the deal was struck.

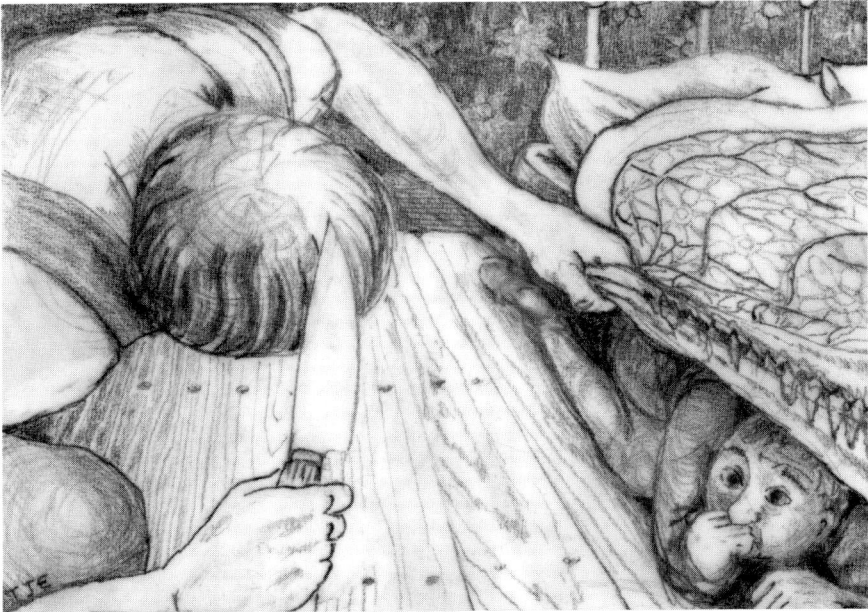

Jack went back home, full of money. He put the money up onto the table, and his mother counted it with him. One of his brothers was watching through a window. The next morning Jack got up and was whistling the day away, when his two brothers came by.
"Where did you get all that money from?" they asked.
"From the skins," replied Jack, "isn't it a fine price for two skins?"

Away home the two brothers went. They killed and skinned ten cows, loaded their horse and cart and set off for town. The two brothers asked a passing farmer did he know such and such a butcher who was buying cow skins for 250 sovereigns each. The farmer replied that he didn't and that whoever told them that, they must be altogether mad. Away they went and found the butcher but only got 1 shilling for each skin. They went home.

Jack was clever. He went a-listening to their house. He heard them discuss how they would come to his house in the middle of the night with an axe to kill him. Jack went home and said to his Mother would she mind if they change beds, as he wasn't feeling too well. They went to bed. In the middle of the night the two brothers arrived at Jacks house. They crept into Jack's room and with the axe pelted, unbeknown to them, their Mother dead.

Jack awoke the following morning to find his Mother dead in his bed. He heard the huntsman's horn, and as quick as a flash he picked her up on to his back and took her up on to the hillside. Jack rested his Mother up against a tree. He waved and shouted to the huntsmen to come over. One of the huntsmen came over to greet Jack's Mother. He grabbed her by the hand, and didn't she fall over!
"Oh cripes," said Jack, "what have you done to my Mother? You must have killed her."
The huntsman was sorrowful. He begged Jack's forgiveness and gave him 500 sovereigns. Jack took away his Mother and threw her into a big deep bog. He went home.

That night the two brothers enquired to Jack as to the whereabouts of their Mother and how did he get all that money.
"Oh," said Jack, "I was walking along the hill with my Mother, when we fell into the big deep bog. Sure, wasn't there, at the bottom of the bog, a little maneen looking after one hundred fine sheep. The maneen said he would swap all the sheep for Mother. We swapped. I took the sheep to the market and sold them for five sovereigns each." The two brothers thanked him and went away home. They killed their wives. On the way to the bog they met a man. They told him how he could get 100 fine sheep for his wife. He said that whoever told them that must be quite mad. The two brothers arrived at the big deep bog. They threw the wives in. Down they went. They called for the little maneen to give them their sheep. The sheep never arrived and the two brothers went away back home full of sorrow for the loss of the sheep, and how they would kill their brother.

The police arrived at the two brothers' house and arrested them. They were hung for the murder of their wives. Jack got the fine big farm, married, had children in basketfuls, lived long and died happy.

That's my story for you, and with the help of God, I'll have another for you tomorrow night, sitting by the fire.

June

Canty's Cove. 1977

The weather settled down and nature's voice changed from the roar of the shore to the humming of the bees and the calling of the cuckoo. The bright, long days were busy with lobster potting in the bay and on land, with 'The Blast of the Potato', sheep shearing and the cutting of turf.

The Blast of the Potato, Shearing and Cloth

On St. John's Eve (23rd June), it was time for 'The Blast of the Potato' of the main crop. A furze fire was lit in the garden so that the smoke would go over the potatoes to bless the crop and keep the blight away. Sometimes a furze bush was also lit and carried over the ridges. Nowadays the potatoes are sprayed with a mix of eight pounds of blue stone and ten pounds of washing soda to a forty gallon barrel of water and then the ridges are sprayed every fourteen days. A few people still carry on the tradition of the 'The Blast of the Potato', as a mark of respect for the old people's tradition.

Dinky O'Sullivan, 1999

A leisurely farmer was once asked, did he spray his potatoes? He said, "I did not, I left them to God and he left them to me, and between the two of us, there wasn't a bit in them!"

The sheep on the commonage at Gurthdove and Dunkelly Hills and on Knocnaphuca were rounded up for shearing by the young and able lads. It was a tough day's work even before you sheared the sheep. The fleeces were sent to Bantry Mill, mostly by boat, to be cleaned, carded, spun and woven into friese cloth and sent back to the family. The mill was occasionally paid in money, but were mostly recompensed by keeping some

Danny O'Donovan wearing a white friese wrapper. c. 1930

of the fleeces. Sometimes the wool was prepared and spun by the women of the house before the yarn was sent to the mill. The women also made the thick, warm friese cloth into fleece pants and white wrappers (long heavy coats) for the men and skirts and shawls for the women. Other times the cloth was saved, and when a travelling tailor called to the house, he was given it to make clothes. Way back flax was grown in a small way and sold to Bantry Mill, where they made it into linen, but the main markets were at Skibbereen and Clonakilty. Ellie Collins (Darby) in

Ellie Collins. c. 1930

Dunkelly West made waterproof clothes for the fishermen from calico purchased at the Bantry Mill. The coats were soaked for up to two weeks in linseed oil, and then the white of an egg was painted onto the outside of the coat to seal it.

In the times when there were heavy penalties for stealing sheep. A boy was up on Knocnamadree (Hill of the Dog or Hill of the Wolf) when he saw a man stealing sheep. The man saw the boy, caught him and drowned him in the Black Bogs by the turn of Balteen. Ever since it has been known as a lonesome place, and caused horses to baulk and shy off. Sometimes, at night, the sound of galloping and whickering horses was heard, and it was for sure that there were none around. The people believed it to be a púca.

Turf and barrfhód

Turf was cut in late May or early June. There are two kinds of turf, shovel turf (black turf - peat) of good quality, and barrfhód (scalps), a sod scraped off the hillside commonage with a grafán or potato spade. The barrfhód would be placed in pairs, propping each other up, to allow a good air flow to dry them and then made into púcáns, of about three feet across. The best black turf of the area was cut by Clancy, who lived up on Knocnaphuca above the lake. It was said that the turf was as black as coal and the best in the world. A turf seller, called Jamesie Brier of East Kilcomane, came around every other month with a pony and cart. Until the early nineteen-seventies, black turf was cut using a shovel like tool called a sleán, at Dhurode, south of the copper mining area. Dhurode also used to be a great spot for blackberries, ferreting and poteen. Until the nineteen-sixties, some Northsiders rented a strip of the Ballydehob bog to cut and draw home turf.

Turf cutting at Dhurode. c. 1942

Turf cutter's rest at Dhurode. c. 1942

Púcán of barrfhód at Gurthdove Hill. 1972

Lobster Potting and Mysterious Happenings

The boats were made ready for the beginning of Lobster potting. The faller and any boat of twenty-one feet or more, was used, but never seine boats. Three boats went out from Canty's Cove and one from Gurthdove. The rope of old strings of pots were repaired or replaced, and the new pots, made in February, were put into strings of twelve pots, with a pole bloc at each end. A pole bloc was a gearnán (good lumpy stone), with two notches made in the middle of the longest sides. 'When leaving port you never went against the sun

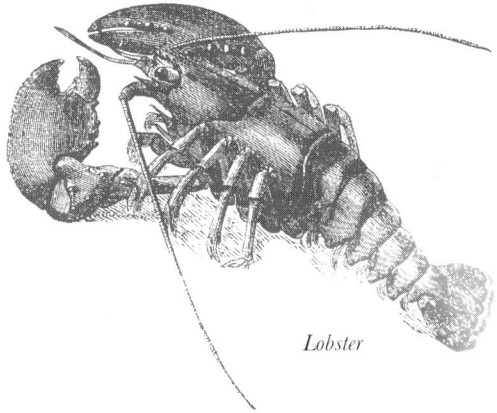

Lobster

or the grace of God'. Which meant that if the stem of the boat was pointing towards the land you had to go clockwise to turn the boat around, or misfortune would surely come. When potting, the men would often stay out for three days, sleeping in the boat for two nights. This would suit the week's routine and allow you time to do a bit of farming as well. The strings were shot and hauled three times a day, on the quarter tides, with the bait replaced every day or as needed. The best bait was salted fish, preferably connor, mackerel or pollock. Lobsters were found anywhere along the shore from Dunbeacon Castle up to Three Castles Head, and you would get at least a couple in every pot. Today you would be lucky to catch two lobsters in a string of pots. The edible and velvet crab, conger eel and the sea urchin were also frequently caught in the lobster pots.

> One June day in 1928, Rick Allan (Richard Collins of Dunkelly), Paty (Patrick McCarthy of Gurthdove) and his son, Jerry Paty, were out potting along the Stakes at the Sound of Bird Island. The bloc (anchor) was cast and they had just boiled some shellfish to eat. There was a knife on the gunnel that, with the rise and fall from the heave (swell), fell out and down onto the sea bed. It was settled kind of weather at the time and didn't Rick Allan see a lobster come into view and take the knife. They decided to shoot a pot, and sure they got him, still with the knife in his claw. There was also a bit of old weed in the pot, to which Rick said that it shouldn't be there, and that something was working below (ground siege) which may be a sign of heavy weather. They decided to shoot their string of pots north of Bird Island where the gear would be safer in a storm. Jerry, John and Jimmy Coughlan of Lackavawn (The Jer Jerrys) were out potting as well. They shot their string where the Gurthdove fellows had just hauled. Rick Allan told the Jer Jerrys what they had just met in the pot, but the Jer Jerrys left their string of pots anyway. Both boats went for dry land. The next morning when they got up there was a strong gale from the north-west, and a great draw at the point of Reen with the heave going to the green (grass). It was a week before they could go down to Bird Island; Rick Allans' pots were fine, but the Jer Jerrys' gear had all gone in the storm.

> When out potting near Bird Island, Jimmy Jer Jerry, was dropped off on a rów (a rock that is submerged at high tide) called Carraigaslí, in the Lug of Meallán, to catch a few fish. The men in the boat went away and hauled the next string. With the grand day they forgot the man on the rów and took things easy. They decided to go up shore a bit to sleep for the night. As they rounded the Point of Spureen into the Lug of Meallán, they saw Jimmy. They went to him as quick as

they could; the water was well past his waist and he was leaning against his fishing rod. Jimmy said not a word and was as white as the froth on top of the waves. The men in the boat shouted at him but he didn't move a muscle; he was frozen with fright. They pulled Jimmy up into the boat and wrapped him in oilskins. It was over half an hour before he could speak, and then it wasn't to thank them for saving him!

Patsy Hodnett (Gurthdove) and his son Paddy were out potting, and Timmy Tim (Timothy Collins, junior, of Dunkelly West) went with them for a spell with his trammil net, to catch a few connor to salt down for the winter. With the quarter tide they were hauling their pots at Bird Island. Timmy heard a boat cutting through the water along with the slapping of oars, and shouted to Patsy to look out for the other boat. Patsy asked Paddy did he hear or see the other boat, to which Paddy said that he did not. Timmy said that they should cut the rope of the string and get out as quick as they could, but Patsy said that they should haul the string, which they did. Timmy made Patsy follow the shore back down to Gurthdove and not to cut across the Lug of Meallán. That was the end of that story and there was no storm or a bit, but it was always wise to pay heed to any strange happenings.

Rick Allan, Paty and Jerry Paty, were potting west of Bird Island when they saw a strange 'fish' much bigger than the boat, which was about twenty-two feet in length. The 'fish' was thin; it was like a giant worm and it came around the boat. The men were alarmed as they had not seen or heard of a thing like it before, and they were very afraid that it could overturn them, so they kept fully quiet and still. The 'fish' kept on looping around, and after a while Rick Allan said that they should bail out the foul water from the bilge of the boat as most fish would then go away. This they did and the 'fish' disappeared.

Timothy Collins (Timmy Tim, junior) at Canty's Cove. 1976

Just east of Bird Island was an area where fishermen have been foretold of changes in the weather by strange happenings.

> Once when Timmy Tim (senior) and his two sons were east of Bird Island potting as the sun was just getting up, didn't Timmy see a man standing at the waters edge. He mentioned it to his sons, who could not see a bit, and yet there the man was, as clear as daylight. They hauled their gear as quick as ever they could, and, with that the sea went to green with a storm.

> On another occasion two men, one being Jimmy Camier of Enaughter, were east of Bird Island potting. It was a grand and balmy night, with not a ripple on the water. The men shot the bloc and went to sleep after having some grub. Before Jimmy was asleep he was stirred by a soft, sweet music coming from the shore. The other man was dead to the world and did not hear a bit. After a short time the beautiful music faded and so your man tried to go back to sleep. The music came again and unsettled him but still he did not say a bit to the other man. The music faded and Jimmy tried to settle himself finally for the night. A third time Jimmy was roused by the sweet music. He had had enough! He woke the other man who had been sleeping soundly, and asked if he could hear anything. He could not. Your man relayed his account of the night so far. That was enough, they hauled the bloc and made for dry land. It wasn't long before the lanch was sounding on the shore, with a strong blast of wind from the south-west!

The Lobster Pond

There was trouble with the French fishermen in the early nineteen-hundreds, who were fishing around the Mizen area, including potting for lobsters. By the early nineteen-twenties, if the French trawlers were caught their gear and fish were impounded, and the French poaching was eventually stopped in the south-west. At this time the Lobster Pond (Celtic Fisheries) was established on Rock Island near Crookhaven, for exporting fish. It employed a number of Northside people and it purchased all the lobsters that Northside fishermen caught. The Pond was owned by a Frenchman, Captain Trehiou, and in charge was Richard Collins P.C. (Peace Commissioner), Goleen. The Pond exported lobsters, crawfish, salmon, scallops and periwinkles. In 1926 over 378,000 lobsters and crawfish were exported, and in the following year 230,000 fish were caught. There has been a decline in numbers ever since. In the nineteen-twenties the fishermen would get one shilling a pound for lobsters. They were packed into crates between layers of butter paper, ice and wood

The Lobster Pond on Rock Island from Castlemehigan

shavings, to a total of sixty five pounds in weight per box. There could only be three cripples (with one claw), and the rest of the box had to be bobs (whole). The French would buy anything you could take out of the sea! The Dutch would buy lobsters and crawfish, but the English only lobsters.

The trawler called 'Rosko' was about 90 tons, and it sailed once every two weeks with fish exports to France. They headed out to the Fastnet Lighthouse, always at night, and then made a straight line for France. Only once did the 'Rosko' ever meet any trouble, and that was in rough weather just off the Fastnet. The mast broke and the ship drifted to Lands End in England. All the crew lived to tell the tale.

Captain Trehiou, who had a peg leg, had to go to Baltimore for two days to order fresh ship supplies. He arrived back to find that the crew had ransacked the 'Rosko's' stores and broken the seal on a now empty brandy barrel. There had been a grand party with the locals and the French alike. Louis, the cook on the 'Rosko', was in charge of all the perishable goods and threatened to hang himself if the seal on the brandy was ever broken. Sure, he was found the morning after the party, hanging from two fathoms of rope. Trehiou was leaping mad and the crew were set to work from stem to stern. Some days later, Francis, a member of the crew, was seen in Crookhaven with cuts and bruises all over him. The Captain had taken his wooden peg leg off and used it to soundly beat the crew. They were tough old times!

Lobster Pond advert. 1965

All fish are now taken to the fish plant at Schull. The Lobster Pond was the last land based fishing depot to exist in the parish of Kilmoe and its closure in 1977 brought to an end the centuries old industry of preparing fish to sell overseas.

Pirate Days

In days past the Mizen coast was the haunt of pirates and plunderers of ships from America and the Mediterranean. Smuggling, too, was big business and it kept the money coming in locally. Ship wrecking also took place with the aid of lamps to misguide the mariners onto the rocks, a practice that carried on well into the nineteenth century.

'The Bold Three Castles Head' was a popular scoriachting song, telling of the beautiful, but craggy, headland, and the plunder and blood of the past.

The O'Mahony 'Three Castles' at Dunlough

The Bold Three Castles Head

Come all you lads of liberty and listen to my rhyme,
I'll sing you a few verses to pass away the time.
Concerning that historic spot, which you have seen or read
Of it's lofty peaks and craggy creeks,
The bold Three Castles Head.

To sing in tenth it's prowess I am at a loss,
To paint its beauty in pictures my pen will not surpass,
Where nature spreads it's bounty, and charms they are all dead
Their beauty will fade when compared with
The bold Three Castles Head.

Still crowning all it's beauties, there in fragrance stands,
Its strong and lofty towers, a pilot to armed bands.
It's bond between the mountains, through centuries of storm,
A relic of old and ancient times,
The bold Three Castles Head.

There is a superstition, an old and fabulous tale,
'Twas used by seafaring robbers who, the ocean main did sail,
The pirates and their plunder they all these did call,
God help the ships and crew who fell into their trawl,
The bold Three Castles Head.

There's more who will object to this and say it is not true
That it was built by the O'Sullivan Beare from the Castle of Dunboy,[1]
Blood stained fields of battle where man for man fell dead.
There is no account in history of
The bold Three Castles Head.

If the O'Sullivan Beare built this place, I'll tell you how it was
'Twas as a protection against the strong and deadly foe.
When returning from the field their hearts with pride did glow,
This was the place to shield them from the reckless Saxon foe.
The bold Three Castles Head.

Now their wars are over and bygone days have fled,
It's many a pleasure seeker who treads the hollow walls,
To gaze upon it's beauties, but it is sad to say,
The mossy, moss grown crumbling walls are falling day by day,
The bold Three Castles Head.

Just like the shamrock one wall unites the three,
So may we be united for all eternity.
The bold Three Castles Head.

[1] It is now known that the O'Mahonys built Three Castles.

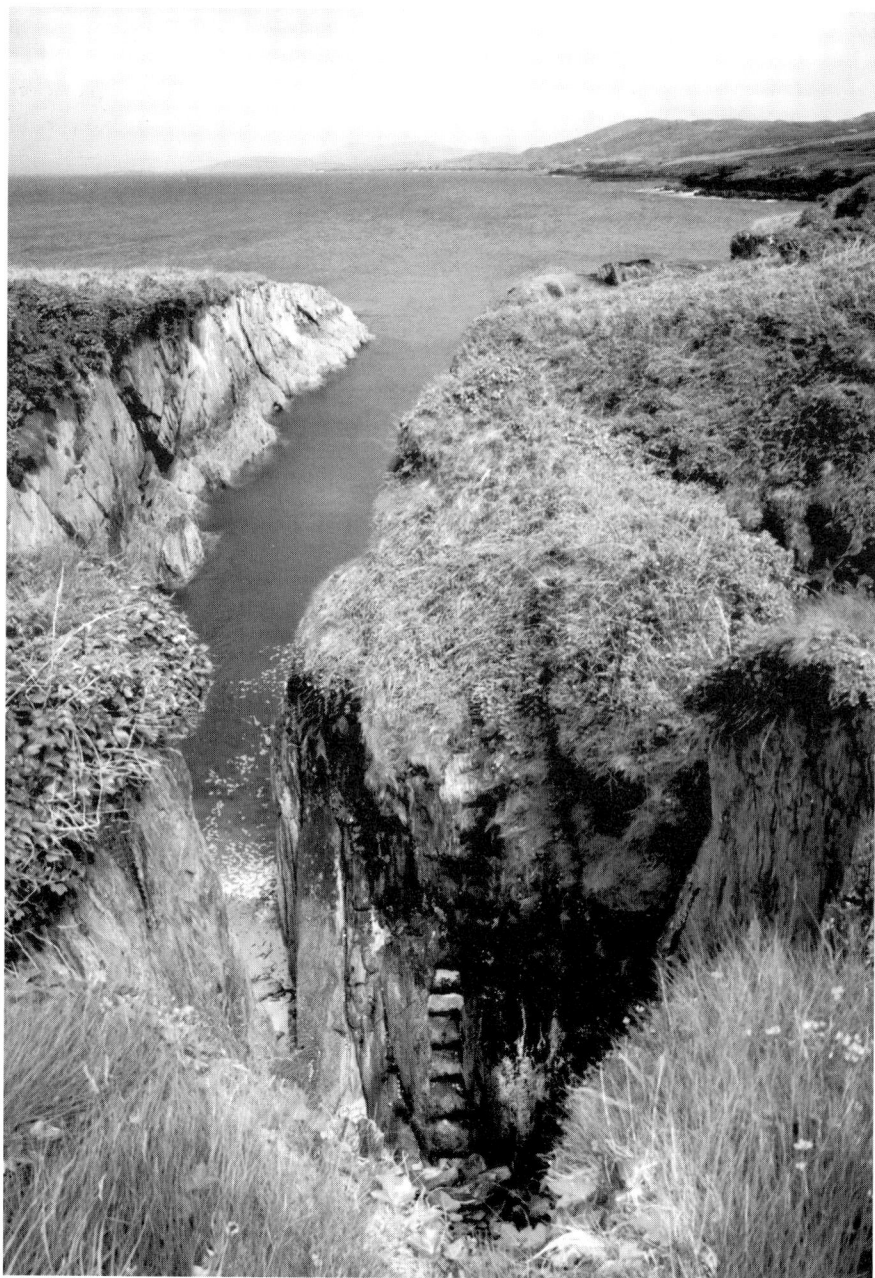

Pirate steps at Cuasnastaighre

Stories of Canty's Cove

Canty's Cove is well known as a lonesome place of unnatural sightings. The name comes from the O'Canty family, who are recorded as being at Dunkelly, which then included Gurthdove and Lackavawn, in the early seventeen-hundreds and before. The O'Cantys were, way back, a bardic family for the O'Mahony's and they intermarried with the O'Dalys of Kilcrohane. The ruins of Canty's house remained until this century, when people remembered that it had a window looking up the inlet to the strand and a door and 'trashil' onto the cliff, on the north side.

Canty's Garden

The local story is that Canty was a pirate and murderer who lived in the house at Canty's Cove. Canty would go out and plunder ships and bring back the goods. Ships captains would come to do business with him at his house, but many did not return to their ships as Canty would give them some special grog that dazzled them. He then showed them out of the north door, which opened onto a cliff and the rocks below! It was also said that he murdered his own daughter before going to a big battle on the south side. Canty met his demise when he invited a captain to his house who had just returned from America. Canty's ways were known to him, and that he had thrown his father, also a captain of a ship, out of the back door and onto the rocks below. When it came to the time for the captain to leave, Canty showed him the back door. The captain was quick and nimble and Canty was thrown down instead! It is said that Canty buried his gold seven ridges from a wall of his house. Many lads have tried digging his garden with the full moon, but without success!

Canty's Cove pier was built in the nineteen-twenties, using stone from Canty's ruins in its construction. Before this time the ledge to the west of the cove was used, as well as the strand, for landing. The new pier would have been bigger, but Mickeen Pairca stopped the expansion of Canty's Cove as he would not sell his land.

There are two sets of steps carved from the rock, one at the west side of Canty's Cove, near the Bone well. The other stairway known as the 'The Pirate Steps' was a bit west along the shore at Cuasnastaighre (cove of the stairs), where now stands what is left of a derrick that was used to draw up sand from the strand below. The pier and boreen from Canty's lane were improved in the nineteen-forties and the ganger was Patrick McCafferin. Two seine boats remained on the pier until they rotted away in the nineteen-seventies.

The Captains of the boats always tied up their own boat. It was late one night when Richard Collins (Ricky Paul of Dunkelly West) was mooring up the seine. The man at the stern caught the painter and the crew got out. Ricky Paul brought the mooring rope through the stem ring in the bottom of the boat and told the man on the painter to pull hard and tie off. He did and went ashore, and with the rest of the crew they made their way homewards. As Ricky Paul was tying off he saw a pair of white hands, as if helping him, at the stem ring. He was not a man to be too alarmed by things like that, but this worked him. After the next night's seining they arrived back at Canty's Cove and Ricky Paul asked the crew not to go straight home, but to wait on the pier for him. This the crew did. The white hands didn't help him that night, but when he got ashore he told the crew what had happened the night before.

More than once, a man has been seen walking along the ledge on the west side of Canty's Cove. On one occasion a whole crew, returning from seining, saw him walking from the north. He went a good distance along the ledge before he disappeared. Everyone in the group was very quiet after that! On other occasions long boats have been seen coming into Canty's Cove, but before coming to the strand they would disappear.

Ricky Collins and his crew came in after the night's seining. It was very calm and still out on the Bay, so they tied up to the pier and said that it would be fine until morning. They were not far up the pier when they heard the slapping of oars in the water and said that it must be a boat from elsewhere. When they looked around there was no boat to be seen, but they could still hear the slapping of oars. One of the older men said that it was the sign of something. They pushed the boat up altogether, and the next morning there was a storm going to the green (grass). There was always great respect for what the older seamen had to say, and had handed down to the next generation.

The Lazy Beauty and the Fairies

There was once a widow woman who had a daughter that was as handsome as the day, but very lazy.

The poor mother was a great hand at the spinning-wheel, and she wished that her daughter would be as handy herself.

Her daughter used to get up late, eat her breakfast before she would say her prayers, and anything she used to do seemed to burn her fingers. One day the mother was scolding her daughter very hard and who should be riding by but the King's son.

"My, oh my," said the prince, "Surely it is not your daughter who is a vexing you?"

"Not at all," said the woman, forgetting herself, "I was scolding her for working too hard; she spins three pounds of flax everyday and weaves it all into thread the next day."

"That's the very girl who will suit my mother," said the prince. "Will you get your daughter's cloak and I will carry her home. Perhaps my mother will make your daughter her daughter-in-law in a week!"

Well, the daughter went away with the prince whose mother was very surprised when she heard all that the girl could do. When the night came the old Queen pointed to a heap of flax, and said, "You may begin as soon as you like tomorrow morning, and I will expect to see these three pounds of flax woven into nice thread the morning after." Little did the poor girl sleep that night. When the next morning came she began to spin the flax, and although she had a nice mahogany wheel and the finest flax you ever saw, the threads were breaking every moment. At last she pushed her chair back and burst out crying. A small, old woman with very big feet came in at that same moment.

"What ails you, you handsome colleen?"

The girl answered, "Haven't I been told to weave all the flax before tomorrow morning. I'll never be able to put it together."

"Well," said the Old Woman Big Foot, "if you will promise to ask me to your wedding, all your three pounds of flax will be made up into fine thread while you are taking a sleep tonight."

It was all as the Old Woman Big Foot said, for all the flax was woven into fine thread by the next morning. "My brave girl," said the Queen when she saw the fine thread, "you needn't do any more today, but tomorrow you may weave all this thread." The girl was more frightened than ever, and she was in great grief, when she saw the second old woman come into the room. This old woman had very broad shoulders, and she told the girl that her name was Old Woman Broad Shoulders. She made the same bargain with the girl as Old Woman Big Foot. Great was the surprise next morning when the girl found a web as fine as the finest paper one could see.

The Queen then said, "Tomorrow you must make all this into shirts and you may give one of them to my son for a present." The poor girl waited very patiently, and she was overjoyed to see the third old woman appear. She had a big red nose and she told the girl that her name was Old Woman Red Nose on that account. The girl made up her mind to be as good to her as the others, for a dozen shirts were lying on the table when the Queen paid an early visit.

Now there was nothing talked of but the wedding. The poor old mother of the girl was there with the rest. At dinner the old Queen could talk of nothing but how happy herself and the bride would be, spinning and weaving all their lives. The bridegroom did not like this and the bride liked it less. The bridegroom was going to say something when the footman came running to the bride and said, "Old Woman Big Foot asked if she could come in?" The bride said that she could and in came Old Woman Big Foot and sat down. The prince asked why her foot was so big? "I was standing at the spinning wheel all my life, and that's why." After a while in came Old Woman Broad Shoulders and sat down. The prince asked her why her shoulders were so broad? And she replied, "It is owing to sitting all my life at the loom." Again in came Old Woman Red Nose and sat down. The prince asked her why her nose was so red, She replied, "That it was owing to being stooped down over the stitching, and all the blood ran into her nose."

Well, boys and girls, there was no more talk of spinning and weaving, and if you go about talking of 'the lazy beauty' it won't go well with you as she has three powerful fairies to help her!

Old Irish Spinning-wheel

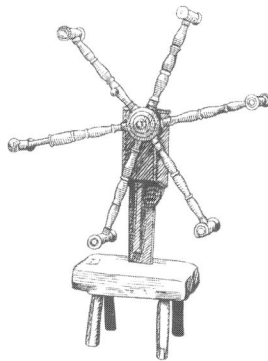

Irish Reel

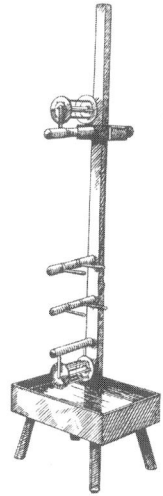

Irish Swift

July

The Hodnett's hay rick at Gurthdove. c. 1940

The King of the summer and with the ripening sun the fine days were spent saving the hay and building the rick. The last of the early potatoes were dug out as the main crop would be ready by the end of the month. The turf and barrfhód were brought in as boats and nets were put into good order for the start of the seine season.

Saving the Hay

Saving the hay needed good weather and forecasting, but when it felt right the work started early in the morning and, with a good moon, could carry on well into the night. The cutting, using scythes, was done by the family, or occasionally with the help of friends. The hay was left for three to four days and then turned with a pike and allowed to dry for a few days. It was then made into small grass cocks and after a week, two grass cocks were turned over and put at an angle on top of each other, into a larger cock. If the weather was unsettled the cocks were rebirthed (moved), and they were again doubled up. If a hay-pike handle was broken, and you needed to burn out the remaining timber, mangolds were stuck on the two prongs to keep their temper.

Tommy Hodnett piking the hay. 1985

The bringing in of the hay to make the rick was a day of great heat, excitement, good food, hard work and banter. It was the custom that a meitheal (relations, neighbours and friends) would help you, as you would, in turn, help them. Two ropes were used to tie the hay on a cart. The ropes were tied to the back of the cart, trailing out behind until it was full; then the ropes were thrown over the top of the hay and tied off at the front. As the cart moved from one cock to the next, the children of the townland would grab hold of the ropes and be pulled along the meadow, and soon became covered in blood sucking tics, and had to strip and pick them all off at the end of the day. If the field could not be reached by a cart, a donkey was loaded up with a 'bundle large' of hay on its back. Alternatively a 'bundle large' was made and a man would lie down on it, face up, and with a jerk of his body would rise himself, with the 'bundle large' on his back, into the upright position.

Making the rick in the haggard was a very skilled job. The rick was made on a platform of pounders (large strand pebbles) and fuchsia bushes.

It was called the berth. If there was any hay left from the year before, it was mixed and spread over the length of the new berth. As the rick grew, the excitement always increased. The men on top would give out to those piking up the hay from down below - that there was too much, or too little, or it was coming too fast or too slow! It

Jerry Collins on his rake. 1970's

didn't matter which way you worked as it was never right!

There was always a good mid-day meal to be had, with plenty of bacon, cabbage, carrots, onions and potatoes followed by fresh cake and butter with homemade blackberry jam, all swallowed down with porter or the tea. It was a more than a busy day for the woman of the house. The

Richard Collins (Rick Allan) and Con Scully (on top), bringing in the hay. 1969

Making the 'berth' for the new rick

More hay for the rick. The authors and Jerry Paty. 1978

The finished hay rick

work and craic would carry on. With the rick quarter made, the 'cos' was pulled all around the base of the rick to the depth of two feet, and sloped out and up to about the same height. Once all the hay was in the rick, the sides were combed down with a hay rake to help throw the rain off. The rick was topped with lúchair or old sacks, and kept in place with old netting. Flat stones, bigger than your hand, were tied with sugán or foxy (sisal) rope, one rock at each end, and thrown over the rick to stop damage from the gales of the winter. Towards nightfall everyone went to milk their cows, but often came back to the house of the rick for more grub and drink. The night progressed with cards, tricks and games and would settle down with gossip, stories and songs.

Jerry Coughlan was the sugán (rope) maker of the Northside. Sugán was made from fionnán grass or straw by twisting and plaiting them from a post in the ground, where there was a long clear space. 'The Rock of the Lines' was the name of the place used at Gurthdove. The sugán was used for fishing, farming and in the making of sugán chairs.

The O'Sullivan's boatyard near Goleen. c. 1920

Preparing the seine

Fishing has carried on around the south west coast of Cork and the Mizen for a long time. Drag seining for herring and pilchards is well recorded from the fifteenth century, local stories of fishing for pilchards are not remembered, although, until recently, there was the remains of a fish palace at Dhurode, which was used in the seventeenth century for pressing pilchards for train-oil. It was said that if the rów north of Dunbeacon was breaking you would get a poor catch, if any, in Dunmanus Bay that day. This could be an old saying as there was a fish palace at Dunbeacon, as well as at Dhurode and Dunmanus, in the time of the pilchard seining.

Ring seine fishing for mackerel started from Canty's Cove in the late eighteen-eighties, when a captain came from Baltimore fish school to show how the nets worked. The crew was out in the morning but did not catch a bit. They came back to Canty's Cove and laid out the net in the Seine Field, and the captain had a good look at it. They ate and drank their lunch and then the captain fell asleep. When he awoke he made some adjustments to the net. They went out again and, sure, in the first shoot didn't they catch a pile of fish.

The seine boats were made ready in late July, or early August, coating the hull with boiling tar and any other repairs that might be necessary. James O'Sullivan of Goleen and Thomas Pyburn and his son Dick from

Toormore, repaired and made boats. The locals would cut the knees from an elm tree, to near the right shape for a boat and then the Pyburns, who were great for the skilled jobs, would fit them.

At the beginning of each season the priest came from Goleen and blessed all the boats and gear. If a new boat was to be launched, the priest came at any time of the year and said prayers over it. A woman should never cross over a net as it would bring bad fishing with poor catches, and if you met a woman with foxy hair on the way to the boats, you would go back home as she would bring you ill luck. Whistling in a boat would bring on the bad weather, as would talk of a priest or a pig. Way, way, back men would go out hunting seals for meat, but more recently they were caught in the nets by mistake. This was very bad luck as it was thought that a seal had the soul of a dead sailor, and a prayer was always said over a drowned seal before returning it to the sea.

There were different nets according to what type of fish you wanted to catch. The nets came from J.B. Roche Ltd. a chandler in Cork.

> The Ring Seine net for mackerel was 100 to 120 fathoms long and six to seven fathoms deep. The seine net had five divisions; the for'ard sleeve, the for'ard bunting, the bunting, the aft bunting and the aft sleeve. The net was deeper at the bunt (the middle) than at the sleeves (the ends). It had a mesh of one and a half inches except at the bunting, where it was three quarters of an inch. The rope at the bottom of the net was called the foot rope, with lead weights every yard, and rings that had a rope through them called the trip rope. The rope called the bunt rope, with the corks on it to hold the net up, was at the top of the net. In the middle of the bunt rope was a large cork called the bunt-cork.

> The Gill net would catch mackerel, whiting, herring and scad. Pilchards were also caught in a gill net, but they were thrown back out as they could not be sold. Patsy Allan (Patrick Collins), caught a load of pilchards one night, put them into a sack and said that he'd sell them as coarse herring. He sold away and met a good market inland with the hill people, towards Schull. After a spell they found out, and ever after he was known as Paddy Pilchard!

> The Trammil net was also called the Bother or Puzzle net as it has three nets of different size mesh in the one string, and would get easily tangled. The trammil was for catching connor (wrasse) and pollock, and the net was always shot in a north-east direction. Many types of fish were caught in the area, including: picky dogs (dog fish), tope, angler fish, the holy fish (john dory), skate, pollock, colefish and whiting. Scallops were dredged from Carbery to Dunbeacon, but by the nineteen-twenties they had been fished out.

The potato crop

Preparing the ground for rape

Root crops, barrfhód and Turf

The 'Ridge of Graf' crop of potatoes was used until the main garden crop was ready at the end of July. Then the remains of the ridge would be dug up, with the medium potatoes saved for seed and the rest for animals. The land was made ready for rape and yellow turnips and they would be sown by the middle of August.

By the end of July, the púcáns of barrfhód were drawn in from the hills by donkey and back-loaders (creel) or cart. The turf was made into a large rick near to the house, or, if the house had a south linhay, it would be kept there with the hens.

The Parish Show

In more recent years, from 1961 to 1978, there was a Goleen Parish Show. The Scullys were the big farmers on the Northside and Jerome entered horses and Eileen often won a prize in the home industries section of the show. The rest of the Northsiders went along for the craic and to look at the displays of horses, cattle, sheep, swine, poultry, vegetables, flowers, apples, cakes, bread, jam, honey and home industries. On this day trotting and donkey races were also held. That night there was always a dance in the hall.

1965

Muintir Na Tire — Goleen Guild

CATALOGUE
OF
PARISH SHOW
ON THURSDAY, JULY 15th, 1965
IN GOLEEN

Price - 2s.

The Time of the Great Hunger

Little is remembered about the failure of the potato crops and the Great Hunger on the Northside, as people have tried to forget, but it is enough to say that those times were as hard as hell itself. There are census figures which show that the population of the Northside dropped from 635 people (117 houses) in 1841, to 291 people (58 houses) in 1851. The worst hit area being Dunkelly East, where a community of 199 people shrivelled to 32 through starvation and eviction.

There was a soup kitchen at Dunmanus Castle, where soup was handed out. It was a black place, and people preferred not to go there unless they had to.

The Reverend Fisher built a school at Lackavawn. Children went for a while on account of the food, but it was not liked and they went back to their traditional form of education. After a year it closed down and the remains stand there still.

The Great Hunger. 1847, Illustrated London News

People were buried at the burial ground at the Poundland and at Kilmoe. Some famished travelling people, who died on the road, were buried near the fairy pond called Bogabarra, on the slopes of Knocnamadree at Lackavawn.

After the famine, horses would balk at Cuasgorm (The Blue Cove) and the people knew only to well why it was so. The priest was called, and he said prayers from the top of the cliff and then went his way. Horses still balked at Cuasgorm, so, once again, the priest was called. This time he was taken by boat from Dunmanus pier to Batoor (the mouth of Cuasgorm), where the priest said prayers for the dead over the water. After that the horses quietened down and worked away fine.

The Farmer and the Woman

At the time of the Great Hunger the people were dying like flies of starvation. There was one lucky man over at Dunmanus who had a few head of cabbage, a couple of cows, and was keeping going pretty well. One golden July day, when he was in his field, he saw a woman and a small girl on the road. As they came on he heard the woman say to the child to pick a couple of cabbage leaves to keep them going. As she spoke she fell to the ditch.

The farmer was a compassionate man. He picked up the woman, that was easy enough to do, and took herself and the child inside. The woman said that her husband and five children had died of the hunger, and that she and her daughter had walked some 37 miles from Dunmanway to find a bite to eat. The farmer said to the woman that things were even worse further west, and that he would keep them for a while until they built up a bit of strength, but that they should then go back home and that things would get better. The woman and child after a time went back to Dunmanway.

Time passed and things were coming on. The crops grew and people started to live again. The farmer forgot the hard times as the years passed away. He and two other men from Dunmanus went to Bantry Butter Market, but for whatever reason it was, the market was not held that day. The Dunmanus men were told that there was a butter market at Dunmanway, so off they went. After getting a good price for the butter they went for a drink in a bar.

One of the men said that they had better be pulling out before the night caught them on the road. The barmaid enquired as to where they were from, to which the reply was that she would not know the place. She said that she might. The farmer replied that they were all from a place near Dunmanus Castle. The barmaid asked the farmer was he the man who helped a woman and child in the time of the great hunger. The farmer said that he was. With tears in her eyes, the barmaid said that she was that child, and that when she had finished work she would take them home and put them up for the night. The men from Dunmanus were treated the best that night, and the next day they struck off south-west for home.

Troubled Times

From the days of the Red Coats, in penal times, to the Black'n'tans, the Northside had their share of trouble. Part of Dunkelly West was known as Baile an Sagart (Priestland), as a priest may have lived there in penal times.

In the time of the troubles the Black'n'tans were sent to Dunkelly West, as they were looking for 'Richard Collins'. It was well known that there was a full handful (five) of Richard Collins's in Dunkelly, but it was also well known that he would not be there. The Black'n'tans went into Ellie Collins, who gave the captain a good long feed and said that they might have better luck in Goleen. Ellie sent them off, along with some hens eggs, to Goleen, by way of the coast road and Lissagriffin, the long way around!

Jer Sheehan, the store keeper from Kilbrown, had to sew his money into the straddle on the horse's back to prevent robbery when going to Bantry to get the store supplies in the time of the troubles.

The only other meeting with the Black'n'tans on the Northside was when they cut a great hole across the coast road at Dhurode to stop cars travelling with ammunitions on the quiet, boreens (small lanes). This did not present a problem, as a couple of sturdy planks over the hole sorted it out.

The Cripples Leap

On the south shore of Dunmanus Bay, near Carrignagapull (rock of the horse), is the little inlet or cove called Trálàraigh. The rocks enclosing this little cove are of the wildest character, singularly broken and irregular in their outline. Rocks and stones, some of enormous dimensions, are flung together in strange confusion. On one of those stones, far up in the strand, is seen the print of a shoe and the ferrule of a stick or crutch, and so the sheanachie's story goes on:

In the time of the penal days in Ireland, a man and his wife and their only son, who was deformed from childhood, were living in a cottage somewhere in the vicinity of Trálàraigh. One evening as the man was out in his boat fishing, his wife was telling her beads for his safety. Their son, who was passionately devoted to music, took down his harp and began to play one of his favourite tunes; when all at once the sound of horses hoofs were heard coming towards the cottage. The good woman, thinking some party had lost their way (as there was a boreen convenient to the place), went to open the door, only to see the red coats, who on seeing the beads in her hand, stabbed her through the heart and she fell dead at the doorstep.

The son seeing his mother dead, evaded the soldiers through some back opening in the cottage, and made the best haste he could to the shore, to warn his father of the approaching danger. The soldiers seeing his intentions quickly followed and over-took him at the summit of this precipitate cliff. The boy, without a way of escape, jumped over and his body was never found. Even up to this day the marks of his shoe and crutch are quite plain to be seen in the stone, although the sea washes over it constantly at high water. The people of the surrounding districts will tell you that when passing that way, on or about twilight, they can hear the strains of music emerging from this little cove before a storm. Some fishermen go as far as to say that when a storm is brewing, from their boats they can see the figure of a boy sitting on this very stone, playing a harp.

August

Curing mackerel at Canty's Cove. Late 1920's

The heat of the summer was eased by the cooling breezes from the Atlantic. It was busy on land and sea, with seine fishing by night and fish curing and farming by day, but there was always time for scoriachting, games and dance, sometimes on Carbery Island or across Dunmanus Bay.

Summer Events

The summer was a great time for dances, fun and trips out on the bay. On Holy Days and Sundays, until 1939, the summertime 'Patterns' were held on the roadside, at Lowertown, Canty's Cove, Carbery Island and the White House over near to Kilcrohane. In the times of boats there were strong links with the people of Muintir Bháire through marriage. The men, especially on Sundays, would often row across Dunmanus Bay to the White House at Kilcrohane for a drink, where the Wills' sister was the wife of the publican Arundel.

Once in the year Carbery Island was the location for a dance and in settled weather the Northsiders could shout across and give the signal to the people of Muintir Bháire to meet at Carbery Island.

As many as forty-five people in three boats would cross Dunmanus Bay to the White House, and a good crowd of men and women from Bear Island would also come to the dances. They were great hearty people. Ann Daly from Kilcrohane and Agnes O'Donovan of Dunkelly played the melodeon.

To keep up to date on events of the day, the men would meet in the evening at various places such as Allans corner, Dannys gate, the Cross of New Road and the Cut Rock. The lads would often have fun raiding Lackavawn and the likes!

There were competitions at Dunmanus for swimming, running, jumping and weight lifting, and you could be sure that the Northsiders were well represented in each of the events. 'Will the Hare' (William McCarthy of Dunkelly Middle), was good at the long jump and running races and would often win and bring great honour to the Northside. It was said that 'Will the Hare' got his name by catching a hare on the run! It was also said that when you blew the whistle to gather the men for seining, by the time you had finished 'Will the Hare' would be at Canty's Cove, waiting!

Wild John Murphy would take the lads to the Crookhaven Regatta which was held on The Assumption (15th August). It was a long pull around the Mizen but a good time was had by all. The Northsiders were great with the oars, but it was hard to beat the Long Island crews in the boat races.

The Raíd on Lackavawn

It was on a neighbouring hillside overlooking Dunmanus Bay,
Those lads set out one evening to give a grand display.
That night came to the corner those lads that wanted fun,
Their leader gave an order that each man must take a gun.
So quickly they got ready and before the break of dawn,
The shots were ringing loudly o'er the land called Lackavawn.

Now Courcey was their target as you may plainly see,
Likewise the Kit Johnnies and those boys that are known as 'We'[1],
Now Courcey stood outside the door, he was in great dismay,
He said to Jerome Scully, "B'gora they'll light the hay!"
Their leader was a brave young lad who never feared the foe,
As shots were ringing loudly o'er the land called Lackavawn.

He said, "Now boys be wary, for Courcey is out below
At his side is Jacky Kit and another man is at his heels
It could be Jerome Scully, I think I hear him sneeze!"
Now Maggie she got terrified when the jennet broke the door,
It was said in Muintir Bháire you could hear the young lads roar,
As shots were ringing loudly o'er the land called Lackavawn.

Now to conclude and make an end these words I have to say,
They did this man no harm nor did they light the hay,
So Jacky laughed and Jerome talked and Courcey scratched his head,
And the lads returned to the corner and went safely home to bed.

[1] The Jer Jerries (- 'We' did this and 'We' did that!)

The Corn Harvest

Most of the people on the Northside had holdings that were so small that they could only grow corn (barley and oats) or wheat, for their own use. The land wasn't good for corn crops. By the middle of the month the stooks were seen in the fields. As with the bringing in of the hay, the cutting of the corn was a great event with a meitheal to help you if needed. For cutting, a reaping hook or the scythe was used. When buying a scythe it had to be sharp enough to lift a penny off the floor. A man followed the cutter, collecting the corn, a sheaf at a time, and putting it out behind him. This was called 'taking out'. Two people followed the man 'taking out' and bound the corn into sheaves with a bind, making sure that the ears on the bind lay with the rest of the ears. Six sheaves were made into a stook and left for a week, then the small stooks would be made into a stook of twelve sheaves which was left in the field to finish ripening until the end of the month. On the last day of cutting the corn, a sheaf was sometimes burnt to collect the seed which was then made into a special ríobún. The stooks were gathered into the haggard, by donkey or horse and cart, and made into a barrel stack ready for threshing in October. The last wheat to be hand reaped for cake (soda bread) was at the McCarthys in Gurthdove in 1969, and it was Jerome Scully who hand reaped the last corn for animal feed in 1974. In more recent times tractors, threshers and other farm machinery were hired in for the day from farmers in neighbouring Townlands.

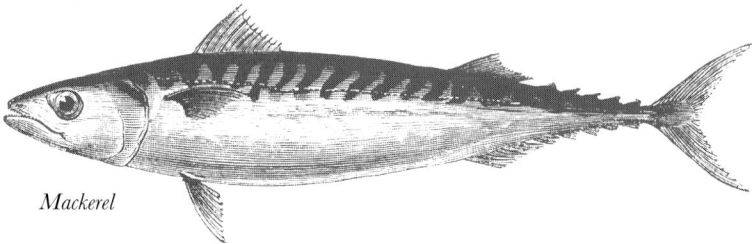

Mackerel

Shooting the Seine

There were two boats per seine net, the seine and faller. The seine boat was 27 foot long with a beam close to nine foot. The golden rule on the Northside was to never get into a boat whose beam was less than one third it's length. The seine boat had five oars of about 17 foot (bow, béal-tuile, aft, bloc and tiller oars). The crew of seven had to shoot the seine net; one man shooting the trip rope, another to feed out the bunt rope, four men rowing

Jerry Paty with scythe for the corn harvest

Tiller

Stern

Quarter knees

Transom

Rib Gunnel Reising Aft taft

Aft taft

Bloc tarft

Main tarft

Beale-tuile tarft

Bloc oar

Aft sheet

Stern post

Stem tarft

Béale-tuile oar

Rudder

Breast hook

Knees

Stem sheet

Stem piece

Tiller oar

Aft oar

Dowels

Bow oar

Keel

The seine boat

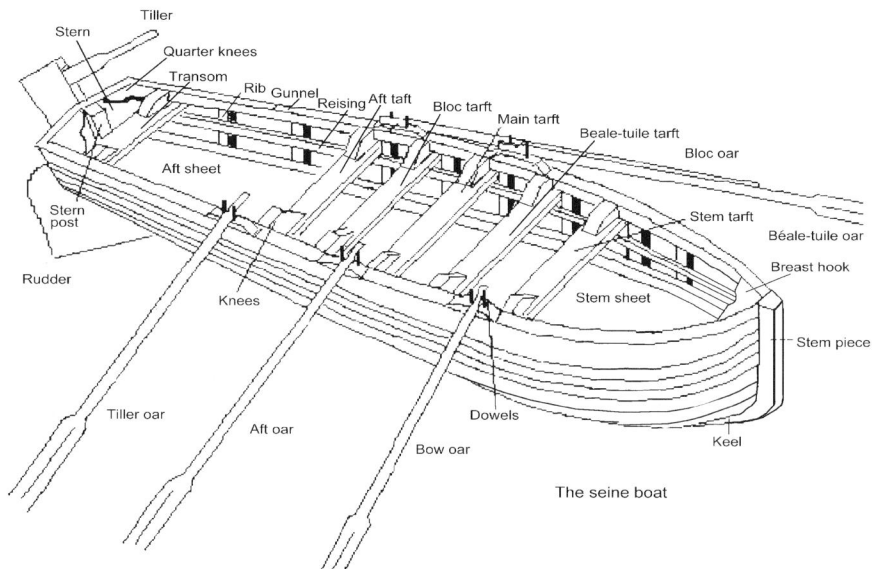

and the huer (master of the seine and captain of the boat) directing the operation. The faller (or bloc) boat was 24 foot long with a crew of five. It's job was stoning and to carry any fish caught. The largest load a faller could carry would be around 5,000 fish. All boats carried a Crucifix and a bottle of Holy Water.

On a dark night if you heard another boat cutting through the water the captain would greet it with a healthy "Goodnight Boat," and the captain of the other seine responded likewise. You would always know which crew it was. Shooting the seine net was a skilled operation with many things to be taken into consideration. At night the schools of fish often went down a bit below the surface. The best time to go out was on 'full dark' (new moon) with the moon going ahead (the later part of the night), as you could see the fire, or barraois (phosphorescence), down in the water. When the huer was ready, the faller boat would let out the bloc (anchor) towards the shore. The faller stayed in one spot close to the shore, as the seine boat shot the seine net. The men on the oars in the seine would pull for all they were worth and, with the extra pull of the tiller-oar, the boat would nearly steer its own course from the west, back to the faller. Mackerel are fast swimmers and often change their course, so stones (never white, as it would bring bad luck), were thrown from the faller to keep the school to the net. Once the two boats were together again, gunnel to gunnel, four men from the faller jumped into the seine boat, leaving the captain of the faller to himself. To keep the fish to the seine net, a trash bloc was jiggered hard, up and down, from the seine boat by the man from the bloc-oar, whilst the other men in the seine hauled the trip rope into the seine as fast as possible. Once all the rings from the trip rope were in the seine, the trip rope was tied off at the béal-tuile tarft (middle thwart), and a duck lamp, made from a golden syrup can, would be lit. The four men from the faller jumped back into their boat and pulled around to the bunt rope of the seine and picked up the bunt-cork. It often took three shots of the seine before a purse of fish was caught. Without a catch of fish, the seine net between the two boats would be overhauled ready for the next shoot. When a catch was made, the crew of the faller worked in two pairs to bail the fish from the net to the boat, using hampers. The seine boat crew, with fingers outstretched, so as not to tear the net, combed in the purse which gathered the fish towards the faller. Two men worked each hamper which held up to 200 fish. The hamper was made from sallies cut on the last November Dark. On a calm night, a faller boat could safely hold about 5,000 fish until there was only four dry fingers, in measurement, to the gunnel. A good catch would be from 15,000 to 35,000 fish and then other fallers had to be called to hamper the fish into their boats.

The most famous night was when 75,000 mackerel were caught. Ricky Paul's boat got into trouble with the big catch, and there was a real danger of capsizing with the full purse of fish. They shouted for help and a second Canty's boat and two from Dunmanus came. All four boats held the net and towed it into Canty's. It took three days to cure the catch. The barrels were all the way up Canty's lane.

On another occasion, up near Bird Island, at Cuasnavisce, the boats were being pulled over with the drag of the net. There wasn't time to let what was in the net, out. Rick Allan had to split the seine net with an almighty drive of his oar. It may well have been a basking shark caught in the net, as with a big catch of mackerel you could always manage to keep the boats afloat.

'If you were born to be hung you would never drown!' There was not a single drowning of a Northside man when ring seine fishing as the boats were a good two feet broader in beam than most other areas, but there were plenty of near misses! One night the men were out and they had shot the seine. Jer Johnny (Jer Sheehan of Kilbrown) was trashing the bloc from the faller to stop the fish from breaking away, and out he fell. B'god, they combed in the seine as quick as ever they could and your man was fairly dazzled, but he wasn't drowned at all! Men from other areas were less fortunate, as recorded in the song 'Drowning in Dunmanus Bay'.

Drowning in Dunmanus Bay - 1916

You mariners and fishermen come listen to my song
And if you will attention pay, I won't detain you long.
How six young men did lose their lives, it grieves me to say,
Near to the shore of Kilcrohane that lies in Dunmanus Bay.

On the 20th of September, all in that present year,
That was the night of a terrible gale through the country far and near.
Just as the sun had gone to rest, they went their nets to cast,
They little thought upon that night that it would be their last.

Those six young men were in their prime and healthy for to view,
Two of them were McCarthys, Tim Spillane and O'Donovans two
And also Charles Coughlan, as the papers tell,
I hope for all eternity in heaven their souls do dwell.

The night was wild and stormy as they ventured from the shore,
The sea it rolled in mountains high against them more and more,
But soon the boat upturned, it grieves me for to tell,
It was there they met their awful fate beneath that deadly swell.

O Lord it was an awful night when the boat and two were found
Close into Bird Island, it was near the fishing ground.
The other four, with deep regret, they fill a watery grave,
O Lord on high be merciful and their poor souls do save.

Now to conclude and finish, I have no more to say,
May the Blessed Virgin Mary pray for their souls this day
And may her Son, the King on high, their parents now console
Who are weeping for their darling men, lost off Dunmanus shore.

A Local Seine Boat Song

The harvest night was my hearts delight to stand upon the beach,
And watch those hardy fishermen as they launch out to the deep,
With nets and ropes of every sort the art of man can know,
With oil skins and sowesters they are decked from head to toe.

Those local boys can ply their oars with a long and steady stroke,
Up to the sheet[1] of big Jack's crew, they say they are no joke.
Eliah in the stern sheet, he there stands steadily.
Where he takes a verse out of his pipe, it all goes in good glee.

There goes the captain faller with a cute sowester hat
He said to Humphry Leary "Where did you get that cap?"
Poor Humphry sees what it took, stands up and threats a blow
And he said, "For your mother's sake I'll break your dirty mouth."

Old Thade pulled stiffly on his oar and the captain he did grin,
"Abagaboy, the gumboil will soon break out the skin."
"Abagaboy," then Thade replied "I tell you that's no joke,
For whilst I have that gumboil there, I'll never ask a smoke!"

They left the quay quite merrily, for I could hear them laugh,
And to their surprise, just by their side, Mike Riley cried, "they're off!"[2]
Big Jack tried to run them through, and the fish made for the shore
And in the rush for to get free, Humphry Leary broke an oar!

They shot away without delay and Big Humphry called them home,
They threw their anchor on the rock, which was soon white with foam,
When those boys saw their seine adrift and began for to joke,
They heard a crack just like a shot, their anchor rope was broke.

One nice old boy came to the pier to make an overhaul,
For Thade was nowhere to be found so Eliah had to call,
When Thade threw off his slumbers he said, "Boys, yer night is poor,"
He thought Toor Island was a boat, and he cried, "They're awful whores!"

The harvest night will come again our shores with fish will teem,
To watch those boys go out again and their captain going by steam,
As the moon goes down beneath the clouds we gather on the shore,
May Heaven protect them from the deep, and bring them safely home.

[1] Bilge boards
[2] The fish are off!

View from the Point of Reen looking west to Knocnamadree and the Point of Spureen

'Cash and Tally Up'

The fish were counted from the boat up onto the pier. Two men would count the fish in hands (three fish). At forty-two hands one man would shout 'a-Long Hundred' and then with the call of 'Cash and tally up' two more hands were thrown up for good measure. A notch on a tally stick would be made. This would give a total of 132 fish. Sometimes there was the very devilment with the counting, by putting the counters astray. On occasions it was known to go a bit far, with strong words and even blows being exchanged!

> Come curers all get ready,
> Have your knives in good repair,
> Come along to Canty's Cove,
> For the fish will soon be there.

The women would now take over the process of curing the fish, which was hard on the hands and many women ended up with bad scars and crippled hands from the salt, and all for three shillings a day. The mackerel were thrown up onto a long table, and split, cleaned, graded, counted and then salted and packed into barrels. With great skill and speed they were split down the backbone, and whoever was doing so received a bit more in the way of payment. Both Canty's Cove and

Some of the fishermen and curers of Dunkelly West, 1928

Gurthdove had streams and the water from them were used in the cleaning of the mackerel. When grading, the fish were sorted into bloaters (big), rags (damaged), medium and small grades, and you were allowed so many of each grade per barrel. The fish were then salted by rubbing coarse salt into them, and this happened twice with the second salt on the tenth day. On the second salt, the fish were packed flat into the barrel, and pickle was poured over the fish until the barrel was full. After the second salting the lid of the barrel was then put down, sealed with an iron hoop and the barrel was branded with the mark of the buyer, along with it's weight and number of fish. The barrels were left on their sides and a hole was made of three-quarters of an inch in diameter, which was closed with a wooden stopper.

Tom Collins (Tom Allan of Dunkelly West), as a boy, would earn one shilling a week by topping up the barrels with pickle after school. Salt added to water made a pickle that had to be strong enough to float a medium size potato with a six inch nail through it. The barrels were constantly filled with pickle until they went for export, when the wooden stopper was hammered home and the barrel stood up. Johnny Hodnett and Joseph Downey of Gurthdove were able coopers, and if any barrels needed repair they were the men to do it. One Cash and Tally of 132 fish would sell for five shillings in the nineteen-thirties. There could be up to 1000 barrels lined up Canty's Lane until November Dark.

Pat Daly and the Devil

In olden days in Ireland in the county of Cork, there lived two brothers by the names of Jack and Pat Daly. The brothers had not paid any rent for seven years when one fine harvest day, the landlord came with two bailiffs to evict them. Pat Daly had a gun. He ran out into the road and shot the three men dead. He searched their pockets for money. Pat Daly went into his brother and said "I'll be going now!" He collected up a sack, a stick and his gun and hit the road north-east through County Cork.

Pat Daly travelled away for some days when he came across a farmer and five men with hooks reaping corn in a field; "'Tis a fine day," called Pat Daly, " 'Tis a grand day for harvesting." One of the farmer's men replied, "We have no time to be talking to an old beggar man like you." "Is that so." said Pat Daly, "Well I don't give a care for any a man of you in a fight." "Oh!" said the farmer, "will you try me then?" "I will," said Pat Daly, "but if you're going to fight with me, you must fight with a black thorny stick, like the one I have here in my hand." A stick was cut, and the fight started. Pat Daly knocked the farmer over the right eye in the first round. He then knocked the other five men, each in the first round. "Now," said Pat Daly, "am I the tinker or the tramp?" He struck off for the road again and had hardly taken a step when a tinker came upon him. The tinker asked the farmer what had happened to himself and his fine men. "You see that class of a travelling man, well in the first round of each fight, he had us knocked out with that black thorny stick." "Oh! 'tis a shame," said the tinker, "to let a man carry a story like that. Call him back and I'll give him a go." The farmer did, and the fight started.

Pat Daly and the tinker man were fighting away, as ever two men could do, with the black thorny sticks. They battled for twenty rounds and on the twenty-first round, Pat Daly gave the tinker man an almighty crack on the head that brought him down onto the ground. "B'god, you're a good man," said the tinker, "I don't think that any a fellow could do that lest he be Pat Daly from Kilcrohane in Co. Cork." "You never know, but I might be that man too." said Pat Daly. He put his hand into his pocket and gave the tinker some pence. "That will buy you some lint to cure your eye."

Once again Pat Daly struck out along the road. He was travelling away when the night came upon him so he took shelter by a rock. The dawn of day broke. Before long he met a maneen coming agin him. "Do you have a smoke?" asked the maneen. "No," replied Pat Daly, "but here's the price of a bit of baccy." The maneen thanked him and went on his way. Pat Daly travelled away eating berries and other things to keep himself going. Once again, he became benighted and took shelter. At the

dawn of day he went the way of the road where he met another little maneen looking for some baccy. Pat Daly said that he had none but again gave the maneen some few pence to buy some. He travelled on and again he passed no house for shelter and so settled by a rock for the night. The next morning he set off and for sure didn't he meet yet another little maneen looking for baccy. "No," said Pat Daly, "I have no baccy but here is some money for to buy yourself some." "Well now," said the little maneen, "I'm the same man asking for baccy that you met on the first and second morning, so now I'll give you back any three things that you may wish for." "Grand," said Pat Daly as quick as a flash, "May my pockets always be full of money." He checked. They were. "That any man I go playing cards with, I'll win every game." "You have it," said the little maneen. "And that anything I let into the sack I have here can't come out till I let it out." "You have it," said the little maneen, "but 'twas a shame that you didn't wish for heaven." "Oh!" said Pat Daly, "I'll have enough time looking for that when I die." They parted and Pat Daly travelled away.

Eventually he came to a big farm where he asked the farmer was he looking for a work hand? "I am." said the farmer, " 'Tis the very thing that I am looking for; can you milk cows?" "I can." "Can you thrash corn?" "I can." "Well, you're the very man that I have been looking for then." Pat Daly agreed a wage. He put away his gun, his stick and his sack, and that was that.

Time passed on and everything was grand. Every morning and evening Pat Daly and the farmer's daughter would milk the cows together and have great larking and merriment whilst doing so. About a year went by, when one day the farmer went to a big town with his wife and daughter, in his horse and trap. The farmer was knocking around town, when he saw over the door of the barracks a picture of Pat Daly and that he was wanted for killing a landlord and two policemen, the reward being 500 sovereigns. He told his wife and daughter, who both thought that it was best to leave him be, but the farmer said that 500 sovereigns was a lot of money and that he would report him. He did.

That evening the farmer's daughter wasn't singing at all. Pat Daly asked what was wrong with her and was she feeling sick? "No." she said. "Well there must be something wrong." "All right, I'll tell you. My father has reported you to the barracks and has claimed 500 sovereigns reward. They'll be coming for you tonight." "Is that all?" said Pat Daly, "Don't worry about that, that's nothing." He went to bed but stayed awake. At about three o'clock in the morning there was a knock on the door. There was a sergeant and two policemen. He shot them dead. Pat Daly went upstairs to the farmer's bedroom, called the farmer and shot him dead too, and said to the wife, "I'd do the same to you only you told him not to. Now see how good the 500 sovereigns are to him!" He collected his stick and sack and once again struck out along the road.

Pat Daly travelled over hills and dales, valleys and mountains, and further than I can or mean to tell you tonight. At the latter end, the day dawned and he set off along his road. The devil was coming agin him. They came up close. They spoke. Pat Daly said, "You're a very smart man." The devil said, "I am." "Tell me, could you go through the eye of a needle?" asked Pat Daly. "I can, have you one?" replied the devil. Pat Daly held out a needle that he had in the lapel of his coat and the devil worked his way in and out. "B'god," said Pat Daly, "you're a very smart man." "I am," said the devil, "I can do any-a-thing that a man has ever done." "Is that so?" said Pat Daly, "Tell me, could you go into this sack I have here?" "I will of course." said the devil, and in he hopped. Pat Daly squeezed the cord. "Now stay there, till I give you leave to come out." He swung the sack up onto his back and away he took the devil.

Pat Daly came to where they were tucking flax. He asked them would they tuck the sack. They said they would. He threw it down into the pond. They tucked away. A good while on one of the men said " 'Tis tucked enough now, unless the devil is in it!" " 'Tis too!' said Pat Daly. "Oh! 'taint?" "Oh! pon my soul 'tis!" "Hold on then, we've another two ponds, we'll give him that as well." They did. Pat Daly thanked them and paid them well. The sack went up onto his back and he struck out along the road again.

The next day Pat Daly came to a forge with four blacksmiths. They had a big lump of old iron up on the anvil that they were striking with hammers. "Tell me," said Pat Daly, "would you put a stroke or two onto this bag?" They said that they had no time for himself or his bag. Pat Daly put his hand into his pocket, pulled out a handful of half crowns and threw them at the base of the anvil. The blacksmiths began to pick them up. "Don't go near that money till you strike the bag." "Throw it up." they said. They started at it, they beat it until one of the men said, " 'Tis beat enough now, unless the devil is in it!" " 'Tis too!" said Pat Daly. "Oh! 'taint?" "Oh! pon my soul 'tis!" "Hold on then we'll give him more!" The blacksmiths broke their four hammers. "Well now we haven't a bad job done of it now." He thanked them and threw down some more money. The sack went up onto his back and away he went.

The following day Pat Daly came across four cobblers a-sewing. "Tell me," he said, "would you put a few stitches in this?" They said they would. The cobblers caught up the sack. They began to sew with hemp and awls. They broke every bushel and awl and one of the men said, " 'Tis sewn enough now, unless the devil is in it!" " 'Tis too!" said Pat Daly. "Oh! 'taint?" "Oh! pon my soul 'tis!" "Hold on then, we have a big six inch nail in the corner of the of the work shop." With the cobblers hammer they pelted it into the devils right eye. It is said to be there always. Pat Daly thanked and paid them. He took the devil away.

"Now," said Pat Daly, to the devil, "speak to me or I'll carry you for three more days!" "Let me out!" cried the devil, "and I promise never to bother you in this life or the life to come." The devil bowled, twisted and turned over the hills and valleys, up and away out of sight.

Pat Daly rambled away through life, but it wasn't long before he died. He went to heaven. He wasn't accepted in heaven. They turned him to hell. He arrived at the gates of hell and told the little devileens who he was. "Hold on, we'll tell the old devil." "Shut all the gates!" cried the devil, "Keep him out! We don't want the likes of him in here!" Pat Daly was talking away to some of the devileens at the gate. "Go in and ask the boss to come out so that I may have a word with him." They did, and the boss came out. "Let me in." said Pat Daly. "No," said the devil, "for we could not get along inside." "I give you a promise that I'll do no harm, let me in for just a game of cards." said Pat Daly. "All right," said the devil, "as long as you keep your word."

Pat Daly and the devil played cards from night till dawn. Sure didn't Pat Daly win every game agin the devil. "Your a very smart man." said the devil. "I am." replied Pat Daly, "Will you give me a request?" "I will," said the devil, "anything that you ask me." "Will you let every soul that's in here out this morning?" "I will," said the devil. "Where do you have the farmer that betrayed me?" "In such'n'such a place," replied the devil. "Do you have a harder place?" asked Pat Daly. "I do," said the devil, "at the north-west corner there's a good drop." "Fine," said Pat Daly, "put him there." The devil opened the gates of hell and let all the little devileens out. They made their way for heaven. Pat Daly mingled in with the big crowd going in, and is sitting there always.

That's my story for you, and with the help of God, I'll have another for you tomorrow night, sitting by the open fire.

September

Father Cotter saying the Station Mass. 1993

It was golden in hue on land and sea. Dunmanus Bay was on fire with schools of fish, making seine fishing the best at this time of year. The carefree children returned to learning in the school. Repairs to the house went under way to see it through the winter or in readiness for the Stations as the Helmas wind arrived and with it the beginning of autumn.

From Cradle to School

Women and men were a hardy breed in those days. Big families were common in times gone by and some had twelve or more children.

> A woman with a large family was having another child. The time came for the birth, and the Goleen nurse was sent for. Things were progressing fast and Ellen Downy (Gurthdove) was called to act as midwife. By the time that the Goleen nurse arrived the lady had given birth to the baby, got up and made the tea! Now there's great fitness and strength of mind and body for you!

The babies were baptised as soon as possible, as if they died before baptism they had to be buried in the Killeenagh Burial Ground and not at Kilmoe or Goleen. The last child was buried there in 1939.

A home made cradle

A baby's rattle made from rushes

From the age of five the children on the Northside went to a school in Dunkelly where a national school, run by John Collins (Darby), existed in 1853. At one time there were thirty-four children attending, but in the late eighteen-eighties there were not enough children to support it, and so it closed. The children then had to go by foot, often shoeless, to the Goleen School, there the girls had their schoolmistress and the boys a schoolmaster. All learnt reading, writing and sums and the girls needlework as well. You could take state examinations if you wanted to, but they cost 2/6d in the nineteen-tens. There was mooching (truancy), but you had to be careful as the punishment was harsh in those times. The children made their own entertainments at playtimes. Hoops, made from old bicycle wheels, were 'driven' along with a stick, but one of the most popular games was pitching stones to see who could hit the mark.

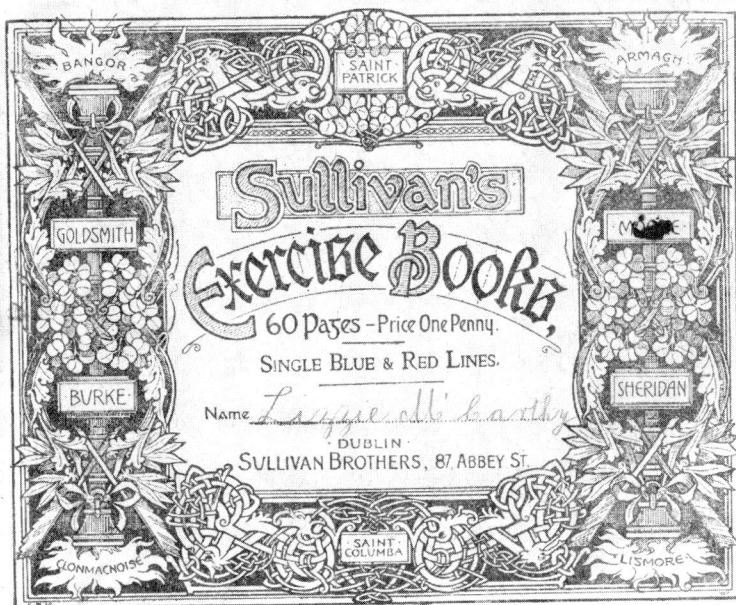

A 1910 school exercise book

Goleen School. 5,6 and 7 class. 1929

By the age of six or
seven, the children were
helping in the home and on
the farm and their First
Communion was celebrated.
This was a big event and
the child wore new clothes
and sometimes received
their first pair of boots for
the occasion. By the age of
thirteen or fourteen there
was the Confirmation and
by then it was time to leave
school. For the older
children of a big family, it
regularly meant emigration
within a year or two for
most of them, but for the
youngest children the girls
would often help at the
home place, and the boys
on the farm and at fishing.

Tim and Ann McCarthy's First Communion. 1923

Fish and Honey for the Home

Until twenty years ago you would see schools of fish in the daytime, close into the shores of Dunmanus Bay, and plenty of them. At almost any time in the day or night, you would be guaranteed a good catch of fish with a line from the rocks or in calm weather from your punt. Very occasionally the mackerel trapped the sprat at Canty's Cove, and the fish could be picked up off the slips!

Jerry Collins fishing in his punt

Fish for home use was salted down in wooden barrels in September, as they tasted better in that month and were thought to be of a more solid nature. The catch from a gill net was also preferred, as the mackerel were bigger and did not have to be sorted like the fish from the seine. New barrels were filled with earth for three weeks, to purify it before washing out and filling with fish. Connor, pollock, ling and hake were often salt cured for seven days, and then put up on a roof to dry out. The dried fish were kept hung from rafters, wrapped in brown paper or fern (bracken), near the open fire.

Rick Allan washed out a fish barrel and left it on its side to dry. The next time he looked at the barrel a swarm of bees had made their home in it. Rick left it where it was and after two years he had a good jug full of honey in it. The time came to gather the honey and there were a good few lads to help him. After the bees were smothered they dug out the honey, and Rick said that everyone should have their fill, which they did whilst it was still hot and fresh. It wasn't long before some of them were throwing out what they had just eaten, and one man never touched honey again in his life. The Northsiders learnt the hard way that honey should be allowed to cool before eating it in any quantity.

Falling Out

You might be thinking that the Northside was a peaceful place, but you could, on occasions, be wrong. The people were tightly packed in and things could get heated. There were feuds and counter feuds between individuals and families all the time. A feud could start over anything; a stray cow, the use of someone else's well without permission, diverting streams, using charms to take the luck of the land, but the most interesting was always a land dispute as they were sure to give a good rising and could go on for years! Two opposing factions could be sitting on the same settle, without giving a single look at each other. Words would not be exchanged except with aid from someone outside the dispute, who would relay the conversation from one side to the other. This could go on for years, and sometimes over generations, until the reason for the feud itself was quite forgotten. It was great craic and rarely, if ever, would blows be struck and you could also be sure that if life depended on it, the two factions would pull away together as if nothing had ever happened.

A man, who was the quietest and gentlest of men that you could meet, one day got out of the wrong side of the bed. He was travelling away through Lackavawn with his donkey and cart, when all of a sudden the donkey balked and wouldn't go any further. He had a bit of a plank in the cart and so with both hands and "Ah, deal mishá, you scourging whore master, so you won't go on!" He brought it down on the donkey's head and it fell down to the ground - dead! The Jer Jerrys' house was near by and so the man called in to ask if he could bury the dead donkey on their ground. The Jerrys said that burying it would take the luck from their land and that he would have to find somewhere else. The man went away spitting fire and cursing. He threw the donkey up onto the cart and pulled them back to Dunkelly! That was some power! It was years before the man and the Jer Jerrys spoke to each other.

The Stations

Stations were held in March and September, when the Parish Priest said Mass in the houses of the area. The rotation for the Stations, in the nineteen-twenties, was every seven years for each house on the Northside, but now with less people around, they are every four years. Getting ready for the Stations was a big event and everything was given a great going over to put a bit of cré to the place. The chimney was cleaned with a furze bush with a rope at each end, which was pulled, up and down, from the chimney stack to the hearth. The thatch or tiles were made good, bad windows and doors repaired and then painted with a bright gloss paint. The outside of the house, along with the inside walls, were always lime-washed. The press, table, chairs and any other wood work would get a good coat of bright gloss paint, too. This custom is well kept up today on the Northside.

The Station Box held the priest's vestments and a bible, and was collected by the next man of the house to hold them. On the eve of the Stations, a neighbour would bring in enough water from the well to last the next day. All the neighbours would come to the Stations. Indeed, if there had been a falling out with anybody, this was a good day to cautiously make amends with a few polite and friendly words to the other party. It would have to be a bad differing of opinion between the two factions for them not to start to make it up, or not to come to the Mass at your home. The table in the kitchen was laid out as the altar, often using two chairs to rise up the table a bit. Mass was held at nine o'clock in the morning and afterwards breakfast was served in the parlor to the priest, the man of the house and the older men of the townlands. Mary Coughlan (Mary Kit) of Lackavawn was always asked to serve this first sitting, as she had the smart way of the people of the

The Station breakfast in the parlour. Father Murphy and Jerry Paty. 1984

towns. As the day went by, all the neighbours and guests had the tea. Often people would stay well into the night with talk, song, baccy and drink, but the night was always respectful for the day that it was.

The Cabin and House

Cabins were single storey, one room dwellings with a door and often without a window. They have not been lived in for a long time. The last person to do so was Jackeen in Dunkelly. Some of the cabins were expanded into small houses with two rooms but most were left to ruin through famine and emigration, or used for animal shelters. There are only two good examples of ruined cabins left on the Northside; the O'Donovans (Dunkelly West), and up on Knocnaphuca, there is Jackeens (Dunkelly

*Jackeens on Knocnaphuca, a pre famine cabin with
the south gable being a natural rock face*

Middle), where the south gable end is a cliff hewn out from the hill. In the time of the cabin there was also the single storey house that had two or three rooms and a loft for sleeping in. It was a tight squeeze, with little height to the walls and, at best, a ladder to get up to the loft. Some of these houses had a north linhay for milk and butter production.

In the eighteen-nineties some two storey houses were built and then in the early twentieth-century, single storey houses were renovated with grant money from the government. The grants varied from £15 to £20, which was a lot of money in those times. Many were raised to a full height second floor, with stairs to get up, and a trap door at the top to stop the draught. Some also had another room added to a gable end and all the houses, except one, had the thatch removed and slate put on. Danny O'Donovan kept the thatch and Agnes, one of his daughters, lived there until she died in 1971.

The O'Donovans at Dunkelly West. The last thatched house on the Northside (Knocnaphuca behind). 1972

The McCarthy house at Gurthdove. Raised to two storeys in 1900

Gurthdove 1968

Houses facing south-east at Baile an Sagart (Priestland) in Dunkelly West. 1975

'Coslows' at Dunkelly West overlooking The Poundland. 1999

The Collins (Timmy's) liked their small, single storey house, and whilst they were still living there, they cut back the thatch and built up the walls of the old house to give a second floor. The new roof was then slated and with that they threw the old thatch out of the new windows and made good the walls.

The old houses were always built in line with the ridges of the land to allow proper drainage, and generally faced south-east. With a new dwelling finished it was the custom to have sheep in the house for one night before you moved in, but more recently when your friends and neighbours came for the first time they greeted you with "May the roof never fall in and those within never fall out!"

'Coslows' at Dunkelly was a building with a difference. It was a terrace of three, two storey houses, possibly built by the landlord in the mid to late eighteen-hundreds. There was a steady stream of outsiders, most now forgotten, passing through it. At the turn of the century, or a bit before, there was a travelling tailor called John Callahan, a dancing master called Harrington and a man called Dan Coughlan, who had a bit of a general store. There was also a travelling dancing master, called Moriarty, who used to come to Dunkelly and give lessons. Next there was a woman who had three daughters who, in turn, had children but were without husbands. Men came calling there and then then named it the 'South Infirmary'. Later, Tim Coslow moved in. He was a bit lonesome and feared ghosts. The boys used to plague him! He was a fat man and used to chase the children. One day, when chasing them, he tripped going over a ditch and the boys had to pull him out, but Coslow still chased them to Danny's (O'Donovan) in his wet clothes. Coslow left in a trawler, and soon after two fishermen and a tailor moved in. The tailor was scared out of the house as he believed it was haunted. He heard noises in the night, but it was only the noise of the fishermen's oilskins, as they returned home from seining. In the early nineteen-thirties a fair came and set up at Coslows, called the 'Hearts Show'. It was run by Doughty and Jones, and they had a 'wheel of fortune' that was remembered ever after! Coslows was lived in until the nineteen-forties and is now in ruins. It had quite a history!

Building Materials

The houses, cabins and outhouses were built of stone quarried from the hillsides. Any good wood taken as wrack was used in building, but the bulk of the timber came from Bantry. Sand for building came from Cuasnastaighre and it was left for a few months to be washed by the rain so as to get the salt out. Small, pea sized gravel for the floors came from Cuasnaghainimh at Canty's Cove, Trágeen and Meallán. 'Yellow Earth' was used for the floors and could be found in many places. The walls of a house were of the double, dry stone wall type, with yellow earth sieved and mixed with water to make a binder in the middle of the wall. All the stones were laid with a slight slope to the outside to drain out any water. You also made sure that 'rivers' (vertical joints) were not showing on the face of the wall, as this meant that the stones were not centred over the joints of the stones below, and the wall would bulge and crack. Jerry Coughlan (Balteen), Jerry Lucy (Ballyrisode), Paty Timmy (Collins) and Jack Mac (McCarthy) were all able stone masons. The Pyburns were good general builders and great at woodwork for the houses and boats. Willie Goggin made cars and also worked on houses.

Miniheens (Marram grass) from Barley Cove and reeds from the lake at Lissagriffin made thatches that lasted up to twenty years, but for the most part straw was used, but you'd be patching it up after five years. Cotter from Enaughter, and later Patsy Paty, were both good thatchers. The thatch was tied down with sugán rope and secured to the wall with wooden pegs, or old horse shoes.

The Fairies Theft

There lived a woman long ago by the name of Mrs. Sullivan. One night her healthy boy had been changed by 'fairies theft', and a fairy child put into it's place. He never stopped squalling and crying and his face withered and his body wasted away, but still he had a strong resemblance to her own boy. She therefore could not find the heart to roast him alive on the griddle or to burn his nose off with the red tongs or to throw him out in the snow.

One day who should Mrs. Sullivan meet, but a cunning woman by the name of Ellen Leap. "You're in grief this morning, Mrs. Sullivan," were the words of Ellen Leap to her. "You may say that Ellen, and good cause I have to be in grief for my own fine child was whipped off from out his cradle without as much as ask your pardon, and an ugly downy fairy put in his place; no wonder then that you see me in grief, Ellen." "Small blame to you Mrs. Sullivan," said Ellen. "Will you take an old woman's advice? and you will get back your child? Put down the pot full of water on the fire, then get a dozen new laid eggs, break them, and keep the shells but throw away the rest. When that is done put the shells in the pot of boiling water and you will know whether it is your own boy or a fairy. If you find that it is a fairy take a red hot poker and cram it down his ugly throat and you will not have much trouble with him."

Home went Mrs. Sullivan and did as Ellen desired. The child lay quiet in the cradle, only now and then he cocked his eye. At last he asked with the voice of a very old man, "What are you doing Mammy?" "I am a brewing aMic (son)." "And what are you a brewing Mammy?" said the little imp. "Egg shells aMic," said Mrs. Sullivan. "Oh!" shrieked the imp starting up in the cradle and clapping his hands together. "I'm fifteen hundred years in the world and I never saw anyone brewing egg shells before."

The poker by this time was quite red, and Mrs. Sullivan seized it, ran furiously towards the cradle but somehow or other her foot slipped and she fell flat on the floor and the poker flew out of her hand. However she got up without much loss of time and went to the cradle intending to pitch the wicked thing into the boiling water. There, she saw her own child in sweet sleep.

October

Horse powered threshing c. 1920

As seine fishing carried on by night, the barrels of mackerel were queuing up Canty's Lane. It was time to bring in or pit the last of the main harvests for the year, the potato crop. As the weather grew with the wind it was time again to look out for wrack and with the nights lengthening, scoriachting and story telling, by the open fire, began.

Willy Birchell's threshing machine (Bill Barry in foreground). c. 1955

Harvesting the Potato

The beginning of October was the time to dig what was left of the main 'field bán' potato crop, and, if on a slope, you always worked from the top down to stop the earth from banking up. As the potatoes were dug, they were graded into large and medium for people to eat, and criotháns (small potatoes) for the animals. Shallow pits, to store the potatoes, the width of a ridge and as long as was needed, were dug in the field, in line with the ridges. If there were different varieties of potato they had to be separated by lúchair (grass) which was used to cover the pit like a thatch roof. Briars were cut and placed lengthways along the sides to bind the 'thatch', and with that, the final coat over the 'thatch' was six inches of earth to stop the frost from getting in.

Threshing. c. 1955

Threshing the Corn

On the Northside, flails were last used for threshing wheat by Patsy and Jerry Paty in 1962. The flail was made from two sticks, tied together with sugán, or foxy rope. There was great skill to flailing with a sheaf placed on top of a sheet of calico to catch the seed. Two men would flail it. Spectators kept well back, as occasionally the rope holding the flail together would break and go flying! Often a child removed the old sheaf and brought the next sheaf, so the men could keep their rhythm going. The winnowing of the chaff from the seed was done after all the corn or

Hamiltons water mill. 1990

wheat was threshed, by putting it through a sieve, called a bórán, made of wood and sheep's skin with holes in. As the corn fell onto a sheet on the ground, the chaff was blown away. Later, threshing machines owned by big farmers from neighbouring Townlands were used. Sandy Hamilton

had a mill by the stream in Goleen for grinding seed, but more often the corn and wheat was stored on the wooden loft of an outhouse until it was needed, and only then would it be ground using the hand-quern or taken to Hamilton's Mill.

With the fire of the sun weakening towards the end of October, the hay, corn, wheat, potatoes and turf were all in, ready and waiting for the winter season. The saving of the crops would be completed with the pulling and pitting of the mangolds in November.

A quern stone ready to grind wheat

Turkey Drives

On Sunday evenings in late October, Turkey Drives started. The women paid nothing and the men paid a shilling. There was plenty of porter, tea, bread, cards, dancing and chat. A card game called 'Thirty-Five' was played until morning. Whoever won the most games took away the turkey, and it was then their turn to hold the drive the next time. The turkey was a well travelled bird and it knew all the houses in the Townlands well! The custom was for the man of the house to play cards, but if he was unable to, he had to find someone to take his place.

> Give them tea so fine and hot,
> Give them butter, bread and jam,
> Give them current cake and buns,
> They'll all enjoy the dance and fun
> While they're at the Turkey Trot.

The Turkey Drives were banned to encourage the use of the hall in Goleen when it was built in 1926, but they continued in the country houses. There was only one raid on a Turkey Drive, in 1946, at a house in Carrigacat. There were two men from the Irish Lights who should not have been at the drive at that time, and with the thirty or so seconds of warning of the arrival of the gardai and coastguards, they managed to get out of the back door and back to the Mizen! All the peoples' names were taken down. There was not a problem

The original turkey

as they all said that they had been asked over to their neighbours for a bit of a chat and that the man of the house had provided the porter for his friends. That was the end of the matter and ne'er a bit was ever heard again. The Turkey Drives went on!

Wrack and Longshore work

Wrack has always been important to the locality. In the days of the old ships it was plentiful but with the modern bulk containers wrack has become scarce. Wrack (and smuggling), for many centuries, brought the Northsiders a means to survive, and one or two luxuries as well. Timber for houses, food, whiskey, brandy, porter, baccy, the means to make tallow candles, and a boat were all taken as wrack but some items, such as cork, cotton and rubber bales, olive oil and later paraffin and petroleum jelly were sold in Goleen and Schull, or to big companies in Cork and Dublin. Much of the timber for houses as well as for presses, tables, settles and other furniture were made with timber that came from wrack, some of which had holes bored in it by ship worms (Teredo) and barnacles whilst in the sea. The wrack timber was regarded of higher accord than timber from Bantry, but then, that might have been because it was free! All apple trees on the Northside were grown from apples taken as wrack. Often cattle were on board ships that ran aground and if any drowned the meat would not be fit to eat, but the carcasses would be cut up and the fat boiled for making candles.

October through to March or April were the best months for taking wrack. Collecting it from along the shore was known as Longshore work. It was dangerous and men lost their lives in its pursuit as recently as 1977. The men would take a boat out if wrack was off the shore, and there was heavy competition as to who could reach and claim it first. Some used to say that wrack carried the bad luck, whereas others couldn't get enough of it. One Longshore man was said to have a particularly sharp eye and he was forever looking out over Dunmanus Bay with his eyes straining the water. The competition was fierce. The wrack never drifted beyond Meallán unless it was in the dark of night. The Gurthdove and Lackavawn men had great respect for the men of Dunkelly as they were often at wrack before they were, despite having to travel from Canty's Cove. Competition between the Northside townlands was good craic but if an outside party, like the Budarís from Kilcrohane, were to be contended with, the matter was more serious and they would all pull together like brothers. Certain spy rocks, up on the land, were known and named as lookout points for wrack, like Cuasanellee, and west of the Point of Spureen, Carrigmor and Turnacarrig. There were many favourite inlets and points for longshore work and collecting whatever the sea brought forth, Cuasawracka was a great spot, as was, towards Bird Island, Cuasabhadra and Cuasnagno. The Dannys' (O'Donovans of Dunkelly) fields were a great place to hide any wrack from the authorities, and the coast guards never impounded any.

THE IRISH DUNLOP CO., LTD.

TELEGRAMS:- "DUNLOPS, CORK."
TELEPHONE:- 1742 (4 LINES)

DIRECTORS:
SIR J. G. BEHARRELL, D.S.O., CHAIRMAN.
J. M. CARROLL.
O. L. DALY.
R. C. FLANAGAN.
H. E. GUINNESS.
H. L. KENWARD.
B. J. O'DONNELL.
D. TELFORD, F.C.A.

THE MARINA.
CORK.

YOUR REF.
OUR REF. EJP/MMcC.

16th.November,1942.

Mr.John J.Coughlan,
Lackavarn,
Goleen,
Co.Cork.

Dear Sir,

We thank you for your letter recently
received regarding the Cycle Tyres that I promised
you when in your district with Mr.Dineen last month.
You will recollect that during my visit you gave me
to understand that you had salved a bale of Rubber
and that this bale was collected by our collector,
Mr.Lynch, Galladoo. It appears now from your letter
that you were not the Salvor but your brother,and as
I informed you in my letter of the 5th.November that
Cycle Tyres had been sent to Mr.Jeremiah Coughlan,
and therefore, if your brother was the actual Salvor
he is the only person entitled to the Tyres.

I regret very much if there has been some
misunderstanding but it has been entirely due to the
fact that on my recent visit you made it clear to me that
you were the Salvor of the Rubber in question. I can
only suggest that if in the near future you should be
successful in salving a bale of Rubber we would be very
pleased to consider your application for Cycle Tyres.

Yours faithfully,
For THE IRISH DUNLOP COMPANY LIMITED,

BUYER.

It was essential for the longshore workers to know at what point the
tide had got to, and a good way to tell was to look to Cold Island
(between Carbery Island and Furze Island). At high water you wouldn't
see the rock at all and at low water there was a good finger of rock, and
from that you could tell, and still can, where the tide was. If you couldn't
see Cold Island you could get an idea of the tide from the amount of
black at the shoreline. Raucs (clumps of seaweed) were always a good
sign, as they often carried wrack.

When out looking for wrack and if none was found, crabs were often taken from crab holes along the shore. At Gurthdove Cuas (cove) you could find crabs under the timber at the wall, by the side of the pier, and on Meallán at South Point, east on the flat in the weeds, or at North Point, going west for Hole Open. Trágeen in Dunkelly Middle was another great place for crab holes. The best way to cook crabs or lobsters was to build a good fire and then open it up, drop the crab or lobster into the greasuc (red embers) and hold it down for a second or two, and then cover it with more greasuc. The taste of the flesh with the fire was turfy, sweet and dry, and was much better than if they had been boiled.

Here are a few stories about the taking of wrack

Way back, a long, long time ago, two sets of clothes, bundled together and tied, were washed up on the shore. The man that took the wrack wore them and so did his brother, and it wasn't long before they both died. Clothes from wrack have not been worn since.

Large bulks of timber were sometimes taken as wrack. On one occasion a very large bulk was seen, but only one boat went out to claim it. The bulk was too big for the one boat to tow. To keep their rights to the timber the crew had to put a man onboard the bulk so that they could go and get another boat without the risk of some other crowd taking it. A good sea was running, and heavy, and your man on the bulk was mighty glad to see the boats arrive back!

Willy Hodnett went looking for wrack early one morning on the 6th Febuary 1881. The Lug of Gurthdove was full of barrels. He came back up as quick as ever he could, and met Patrick McCarthy and cried, 'Paty, Paty, Paty, the Lug is full of barrels of pigs!' There were barrels of cured bacon that they kept, cotton bales which were used for caulking old boats, olive oil that was grand for frying meat and some of it was given to cattle, but the palm oil they sold. All the wrack came from the 'Bohemian', a ship that went aground at the Mizen with the loss of 35 men, including the captain.

A life boat from the ship 'Margaret Mitchell (Glasgow)' was wrack taken at Trágeen by the Will family. The boat was nick-named 'Maggie'. It was a handy boat with a good beam, and was great for taking the barrels of salted mackerel from seining out to the ships anchored in Dunmanus Bay, that were bound for Liverpool and the Americas. 'Maggie' ended her days in the loft of the cow shed at the Wills where, until the nineteen-sixties, she was used for storing grain.

EIRECOT COTTON CO. LTD.

DIRECTORS: H. D. BRISCOE (CHAIRMAN) W. BRISCOE SECRETARY R. BRISCOE L. GLASERSFELD (CZECH)

"WADDING - DUBLIN"

TERMINUS MILLS · VERGEMOUNT
CLONSKEAGH
D U B L I N
E I R E
CODES: A.B.C. 5th ED
AND BENTLEYS

BALLSBRIDGE 888

OUR REF WT/VHW. 6362.

YOUR REF

DATE
26th February 1943.

Mr. John J. Coughlan,
Lackavawn,
Goleen,
CO. CORK.

Dear Sir

We thank you for your letter of the 22nd inst. enclosing
sample of Cotton of which you state you have 15 cwt. Although we
are not users of this particular class of Cotton, we are prepared
to buy same, and we shall be glad to know:

(1) Price per lb. required.

(2) Whether Carriage Paid or not.

(3) How the material is packed.

(4) The general condition of the material i.e.
is the whole of it equal to the sample you
have sent us, or has some been damaged by
water; and whether it is waterlogged yet.

You will understand that it is impossible for us to offer
you a price for same without having actually inspected the bulk,
and it is too small a quantity to warrant the sending down of a
Representative to examine it. If you will be good enough to answer
the above particulars, we will give the matter consideration as to
whether we can purchase same.

Yours faithfully,
EIRECOT COTTON CO. LTD

Cuasawracka at Lackavawn (cove of the wreckage) was a good spot
for wrack. One time a barrel of porter was found and tar-buckled
up with ropes, and another time twenty-eight barrels of olive oil
were taken, and a man in Kinsale gave two pounds apiece for them.
The reward was the best part of one man's share for a season of
seining. Brandy West and Brandy East, near Bird Island, were other
coves, where, as the name suggests, barrels of brandy were found.
Once the Coast Guards caught a man with an 80-gallon barrel of
whisky. They were merry for many a night after!

Early in this century there was an English Coastguard, a decent sort of man, who lived in Goleen. He used to watch for wrack and one day he told a man in Dunkelly that an 80 gallon barrel had arrived at Barley Cove. "Don't be afraid of me, but if someone tells me, I have to report it to Schull." The Northside lads went for the barrel. They drew out the whiskey into a couple of smaller barrels and anything else they had handy. Away with them they went and hid the barrels in a field where they could not be found, and drew out of them, as and when they wanted. The Schull Coastguard eventually came to collect the barrel at Barley Cove, but it didn't do much good as the barrel was found to be full of salt water!

During the First World War it was good for wrack and there must have been many ships go down; may the sailors rest in peace. One fine day, Northsiders woke early in the morning to find Dunmanus Bay full of barrels. They were all pushing, bobbing and banging into each other like corks. The barrels were full of olive oil, lard, apples, bacon, palm oil, bales of rubber and all sorts of other things. Wrack that was surplus to the needs or didn't have a use on the Northside was sold on the street in Schull, where a good market was met.

In February 1941, in Dunmanus Bay, a raft was taken on a sharp, hardy day, with the wind pushing from the north-west and a good sea running. Timmy Tim (junior) put out his faller as she was a good boat on a hardy day. The crew, of two Jer Jerrys, Jacky Kit, Pad Long and Mike Danny, had a heavy pull that day. The men went out of the mouth of Canty's Cove and turned west outside of Pointamór. The boat took in a good sup of water, and Timmy was bailing out as fast as it was coming in. Mike Danny was on the steer in the stern and when he saw a heavy sea coming agin him, he'd tip his cap and say, "Gracious God men, hold her to it, for a weighty sea is a-coming!" They hitched onto the raft, and with that there was a boat from Kilcrohane upon them, but they kept it at bay. With the heavy day they were carried down east to Trágeen, and they had a tough pull back to Canty's Cove. There were tablets, chocolate, oilskins and first aid equipment in the raft. The name on the tablets was 'Horlicks' and it was said that if you ate one you would hardly need any food for the rest of the day. Paddy Mac (McCarthy) and John Cotter came out from Schull. Paddy Mac bought the bolts, and the timber was shared equally between the crew. Cotter, although he bought nothing, struck a better deal as he made a match with Mary Timmy (Collins) of Dunkelly that day!

Fairy Forts and the Past

Fairy forts, souterains and standing stones have always been left well alone, as no good would come to you if you interfered with the little people in anyway. Only once was a standing stone removed by someone in Lackavawn, and when they returned the next day it was back to where it had been before. There was ill luck for him in that field, ever after. The blocking of fairy and Mass paths was considered wrong and a foolish thing to do.

> One day a man blocked a fairy path, but when he returned the next day it was back to how it was in the beginning. The man was tough, and he made changes to the path for the second time. He came back the next day only to find it open yet again. The man was bold out, and for the third time he blocked the way. The next day he rambled along the fairy path. It was a grand fine morning and he quite forgot himself and the work that he had done the day before. Didn't your man try to walk straight through where he had blocked the path? He fell down and broke his leg. Somehow your man got home alright, and he swore that he would open the fairy path and leave it that way, but there was little need for that, as it was already done!

Queer things happened in the past when the fairies and púcas were about, for instance, you could get stuck inside fields at night. It was more than one person that gave a good spell at it, often until the rising of the sun. All the gaps would disappear and if you climbed a ditch and jumped down the other side, you would find that, as hard you tried, you always jumped back into the field that you had just come up from! It was said that the little people were after having a bit of fun.

Luminous animals, something between a sheep or a dog, have been seen along Canty's shore and at Drishane Cross. On Knocnaphuca, as well as at other places, moving blue lights have been sighted.

> One night Pat McCarthy was on his way back from John-J's house. He was south of Catherine Murphy's and near to the Courceys' house when he saw a light to the east. He looked at it a little while and decided to go and find it. He went in over the ditch and after about six steps he lost it. Pat went back out, up onto the road and saw it again and decided to have another drive at it, so he went after it again. Once more, Pat lost the sight of it so he went back up to the road and sure enough there it was, clear to be seen. It headed north to north-west. Pat kept watching the light until it went out of his sight and he then tore the ditch so that, with the dawn of day, he could have a better reckoning. The way that he figured it was that the light went north of Hodnett's sleabh and then down into Garranabilla, and then away, north-north-west and out of sight.

Bronze Age stone circle, Dunbeacon

Standing Stone, Lackavawn

Standing Stone, Dunmanus East. (Two stones fallen)

Cliff edge fort and souterrain, Dunkelly East

The Devil himself! Patrick McCarthy, emerging from Pollgorm on Lackavawn Hill

Johnny Mosseen, foreteller of the future

Johnny Mosseen (John Downey of Gurthdove) was the last of the ancient tradition of seers. He had the old way of talking to the little people. Often at night he would go into a trance, not seeing or hearing anyone, and walk out of the house. It was best to leave him be when he was out walking with the fairies. Johnny Mosseen foretold a pile of happenings, but he was ne'er a bit of value to himself.

> After Mass one Sunday, Johnny Mosseen forecasted that a ship would go down at the Mizen during the time that the fog signal station was being built. And it happened. Mosseen was right, but it wasn't one ship that went down, but three. The 71 ton steam trawler 'Ribble' sank on 26th of May in 1906, and all the crew were saved. The 'Manaos' an 82 ton steam trawler sank on the 1st of October in 1908, with the loss of the mate. The 'Irada', one of the largest vessels in her time (8124 tons, 501 feet), ran aground and sunk on the 22nd of December in 1908. The 'Irada' had a cargo of cotton, and eight crew, including the captain, were lost.

> A lad in Goleen was hit by a horse on the head. A doctor came from Cork and operated on him in Goleen. The doctor said that straw should be put on the road so as the metal bands on the cart wheels would not make any sound, but it was thought that the lad was

beyond repair. Johnny Mosseen said that he had spoken to the little people and told them of the mark that was on the boy's head. The little people said some few words over the lad, and told Mosseen that the boy would be as good as ever, and indeed he was.

In 1906 there was an earthquake in San Francisco. Two men from the parish of Goleen were there at the time. The mother of one of the men was fearful for her son's life, and so she went to Johnny Mosseen who said that he would tell her about him tomorrow night. When she went back to Johnny, he said that her son was fine, and that there was nothing to worry about. Three weeks later the mother got a letter and money from her son in America and everything was grand.

The Gurthdove seine had been out a few nights without catching any fish. They came ashore and were heading for home when they met Mosseen, who asked if they had a haul of fish, to which the men replied that nothing was doing. He said that it was hard to catch fish when you left them behind you. One of the crew enquired as to where they should be looking. Mosseen said that they should shoot the seine just east of Pollamúislee. The men went and shot the seine and took a purse of fish.

Johnny Mosseen fell asleep in a field near Goleen after watching a football match, A lad who was going for cows woke Johnny, who said that the milk of the parish would be spilt in that field. It was some thirty-five years later, in 1959, that the Creamery at Goleen was built there.

One night, Andy Donovan (Ballydevlin), came in from fishing to Canty's Cove. It was a dark, dark night and he met Mosseen in Dunkelly. Andy said that he was afraid of going across Knocnaphuca, so Mosseen gave him an elder stick and told him not to lose it. They parted company and after a few steps Andy threw the stick over a ditch. It wasn't long until he was lost altogether, but he kept going. At dawn he found himself in Corlacka. He made his way home. The following night Andy met Mosseen. He kept quiet and said nothing about going astray, but Mosseen told him where he had been that night and that it was a shame that he didn't keep the stick that he had given him, as it would have served him well. Andy never received another elder stick from Mosseen but other people did, and to be sure, they kept them.

Two lads went for sand, Dinny Long and Tom Hodnett. Their car overturned and they were badly hurt. Johnny Mosseen asked after the two lads from a neighbour, and was told that Tom was fairly good, but Dinny was still upset. "Don't worry about him, he'll travel many a boreen," said Mosseen, "but Friday will tell the tale for Tom Hodnett." And so it was. Tom was dead by Friday and Dinny lived to a ripe old age.

There was a man who lived in Canawee, just to the west of Barley Cove, who said that he was kind of dry after the day before and so he would head out for Crookhaven for a sup to drink. Johnny Mosseen, as quick as a flash, replied that it was a shame that the man wouldn't live long enough to see plenty of drink just below him. That is where the Barley Cove Hotel is now situated.

There was a fellow at the Skibbereen court who was just after registering land. Mosseen was there and asked where was he from. The man replied that he was from Barley Cove, to which Johnny Mosseen replied that someday the strand would be black with people. You should see it on a bank holiday today, but there again, perhaps you have!

Barley Cove Beach c. 1970

The Fire of Bones

In olden days in Ireland, there was a king and in his reign there was a law made that whenever a man came to the age of 70 years, he was to be burned on a fire of bones. So that was the law of the land.

The king had twelve men working for him collecting bones. It came to pass that one of the king's men had a father who was coming to the age of 70. Your man thought that it was a sorry thing that his father was to be burnt on the fire of bones. So, the king's man took his father up onto his back and travelled to a cave by the sea for to hide him. Your man went every night to take the old man food and baccy, and to see how he was getting on.

One evening before leaving the king's fort, the king gathered his men to ask them if they could answer a problem that he had. The king had a tree knocked down and a bit of a stickeen made from it. He had it cut and planed to four inches all around. "Now," said the king, "can any a man of you tell me how to grow it in the ground? If you can I'll give you a sovereign." B'god, your man went away back to his father and told him what the king had said. "All right," the old man replied, "I know that the king is trying to find me, but no matter, a sovereign 'tis a lot of money. You have children and are finding it hard to make ends meet." The old man told his son what to do. The next morning the king asked if any a man had earned the sovereign. Your man stood up and said that he had, and that if the king was to throw the stickeen into a stream, the end to put into the ground for to make it grow would be the end that turns against the flood. "That's very good," said the king, "you must be a learned man. Here's your sovereign."

Time passed away, and once again the king called for all his men. "Who ever can answer me this," said the king, "will earn himself five sovereigns; Who am I the fondest of? Who is the fondest of me? And who is my greatest enemy?" Your man was a bit confused and so went to see his father. "How well the king knows," said the old man, "that only an old man of 70 could answer that, but no matter, 'tis a good bit of money. Tomorrow morning, get your horse and put your son up in front of you, your wife up behind you, and call your dog beside you." The old man then told him what to say. "Well now," said the king, "have any of my men earned the money, this fine day?" Your man could see that none of the other men had the outfit for the reply. So he repeated what his father had said; "That I am the fondest of my son and however often I beat my dog, he is the fondest of me, and that my wife is my greatest enemy." The man's wife leapt off the horse and with a great roar said, "And to think that your father has been hidden away in the cave for the last six months and I haven't said a word." "That will do grand," cried the king, "Here's your five sovereigns, Go and collect the old man."

After a week, the day of the bonfire came. People from all over the land, from near and afar, were gathering for the great day. The son was mournfully travelling along to see his father being burned up. Along his way he met an old travelling man. "Are you on the way to the fire of bones?" said your man. "I am," replied the gentleman of the road, "and I understand that it is the custom to sing a song or tell a story, ne'er a one of which I can do. Will you help me?" "I will," said the son, "I shall tell a story for you."

The fire was a blazing and lots of songs and stories would be told before the old man would go to the bonfire. It was not long before the travelling man was called by the king. He gave his excuses for not being able to do one or the other, but that he had a man to take his place. "Better still," said the king. So your man stood up and said, "Before I begin my story, may it be that if any man interrupt me, that he be put on the bonfire instead of my father?" His wish was granted and so his story started.

"Myself, my mother and my grandmother set the whole of Ireland to corn one day. The next morning, when we awoke and got up, it was ripe. We got our three hooks and started reaping away. My grandmother stayed south-west, my mother went east and I went north-east. We were reaping away when all of a sudden I startled a hare. I fired my hook at it and it fastened into it's leg. It ran to my mother and she pelted it to my grandmother, and we went around in this fashion until we had all the corn cut down. The next day we sheaved it, put it up into stooks and then threshed it. Now that was a good days work! The following morning I sewed a sail up and put the corn into it. I threw the sail and all onto my horses back and struck out for the market.

I was going over a big river when my horse was knocked over. What had happened I didn't know. I looked, my horse had four shoes and there were, on each shoe, six nails and on every nail there was a salmon stuck fast. So I had a lot of salmon for the market, but my horse had been badly skinned on the back and to take such a load was very hard. There was a sheep near by so I caught it, killed it, skinned it and put it up on my horses back. The sheepskin wasn't staying on so well so I cut a biteen of a briar and twisted it about my horse. That was fine and do you know that every year after that ten packs of wool came off the sheep skin, and seven bushels of blackberries from the briar . . . . . .!"

"B'damned," yelled a big whiskery fisherman, "you're a blasted liar, and you've been telling us lies all the time." "That will do," said the king, "that man's for the bonfire." So the fisherman was burnt and your man's father was taken home safe.

That's my story for you, and with the help of God, I'll have another for you tomorrow night, sitting by the open fire.

November

Hill fire control

The month opened with Snap-apple night and tales of pucás and little folk. From the rising of the moon on November Dark the mackerel would make their way to deeper water; it was the end of the seine season. With the crops all in and hill grazing finished, fires were set on the hills and preparations made for the winter. There was little employment for the months ahead.

Snap-apple night

Snap-apple night (Halloween, the eve of All Saint's Day, 1st November), was a night of mischief for both children and the púca! The following day was All Souls Day (2nd November), and was when prayers for the souls of the departed were always said. On the Eve of All Souls Day a candle was placed at the kitchen window and left to burn out, to guide one's dead family who came visiting on that night.

A grand feast was prepared for the evening meal of Snap-apple night, with a little bit of everything you could ever want; bairín breac (fruit cake), hazel nuts, blackberry and apple pies. Trials of strength and agility, as well as riddles and tongue-twisters, were always part of the night's games. You can be sure that if anyone didn't meet the mark, they'd suffer! It was a good thing to have a witty tongue and strength of mind and body with you that night. Sometimes the sconcing could lead to horse-play of a more physical nature.

The first game of the night was always 'Snap-apple' when an apple was hung from a beam in the kitchen and all the children took turns to 'snap' the apple. Sometimes the apples were put in a half barrel of water and you had to take one out with just your teeth, with your hands behind your back. A favourite game for the older lads was 'Hop, Skip and Jump', and a good distance could be travelled by the person who had practised. Another game was to lift a chair from the ground, with the use of one hand, holding the bottom of one of it's legs, and the wrist was not allowed to bend. If anyone was particularly good at any of the games, then the others would torment them while they were performing their feat of strength or agility. Once the young people had worn the devilment out of themselves, they would settle down by the open fire for stories of púcas, leprechauns and other small folk.

Narry the Bog

One fine Halloween, Neddy Hodnett (Gurthdove) was crossing the land on the way back from scoriachting, when he came across a Narry the Bog (a heron) at Hodnett's Sleabh. He caught it and put it under his coat. Neddy knew that Dan Thade Coughlan was out scoriachting and he also knew what route across the fields Dan would take, so he hid in a béillic. It wasn't long before Dan came from the east, and as he passed the béillic, Neddy knocked a screech out of the Narry.

Dan leapt out of his skin with fright and with a roar he leapt over the ditch and away out of sight. Dan didn't take long to arrive home and he told everyone that he had met the devil himself, coming agin him! Dan did not leave the house, day or night, for a week and in the end Neddy had to go and tell Dan what had taken place that night. He took some convincing!

The Púca of Knocnaphuca

The old people would feed the Púca of Knocnaphuca on 'Snap-apple Night', or indeed, whenever one had a call to travel up the hill. It was the wise person that fed the Púca the night before going up. Milk and cake would be put on a plate and left outside the house and by the next morning the food had always gone!

The Púca of Knocnaphuca was half horse and half human. One late Snap-apple night there was a young lad out walking the road when he heard a strange, sweet music coming from the hill. He went up and saw the Púca playing on a whistle. As soon as the lad had put eyes on it, it stopped playing and caught him. Away the

Púca went to the top of the hill, where a crack opened up in the rock. In they went. They went twisting and turning down through tunnels until they entered a chamber full of gold. "Now," said the Púca, "you are mine!" . . .

The next morning the boy was found on the road by the Long Bog. His hair had turned white and he could not speak a word ever after.

The leprechaun

In olden days in Ireland there lived a big, rich man who had a lot of gold, but was afraid that it might be stolen. The rich man had a little man who helped him, and asked him to hide his gold. And so it was that the first leprechaun took the gold up into the hills and buried it in a croc.

One day a boy was going to the mountain for his cows at sun rise when he saw a leprechaun mending his shoes, and he stole up on him and caught him and asked him for the gold. The leprechaun said "Look behind you and you shall have the gold." The boy did so, and when he looked back the leprechaun was gone. Time passed on and the boy caught the leprechaun for the second time, he asked him for the gold. "Follow me," said the leprechaun. The boy followed the leprechaun to a river and was told to cross it, but the boy said that he could not and that the river was too wide. The boy looked to see if there were any stepping stones to cross, and as he did so the leprechaun disappeared. The boy never saw him, ever after.

The Close of the Farming Year

Fires on the hills were set from November to April so as not to interfere with the grazing of animals or the nesting of wild birds. Commonage was burnt every five years, as it was good for grazing and improved the quality of the barrfhód. There was a system in the burning and different areas of the hills were burnt in different years. The wind direction was important, as you would want the fire to go to the fire break of the previous year. It was also best not to have it too dry, otherwise the whole thing could get out of control.

A pig or a goat, was always shown the knife in November. Although not knowingly linked to Martinmas (11th November), the killing of the pig may well have been related to this occasion. As many pots as possible were boiled up with water to shave the pig after the slaughtering. The pig was hung for one day and then cut into joints, packed with salt and put into a pickle of the same strength as for the fish. The corned bacon was kept until Christmas before eating.

Twigs and Wild Rods were cut as close to November Dark (new moon) as possible as they would have the most bend in them. They were harvested from as far away as Ballycommane, but most houses also had a willow bush or two. A hook, not a saw, was used to cut the willow, as a clean cut would allow them to grow again. The twigs and rods were stored until February, when baskets of all sorts were made.

> Clancy Cricky had a piggy
> He put him on the clover,
> The piggy died and Clancy cried
> And all the fun was over.

The Tally of the Seine Season

With the rising of the moon from November Dark the mackerel made their way to deep water; it would be the end of the seining season.

Most of the barrels of fish were collected by ships from September onwards. Limerick Steam coasters and ships from England and America anchored offshore, and the barrels would be taken to them. The faller boats took five to eight barrels per trip to the ships. They were hauled up by a derrick, two at a time, into the hold. Often 300 barrels would be loaded onto one ship. In the late eighteen-eighties, barrels of fish were taken to Schull by horse and car in September. The car would take five barrels but could only manage three up Canty's Lane. Two were taken up first and dropped off, and then they went back down for the next three. At Schull, the fish barrels were dropped off and a ton of salt was brought back to Canty's Cove. You would get ten shillings for the round trip. Later on, a two ton lorry, that travelled at ten miles an hour, picked the fish up from the top of Canty's Lane.

> On one occasion Jim Will and his brother Bill were loading a ship when a storm blew up. They were in the 'Margaret Mitchell', and with the big heave and squall, they were taking on water and had to throw six barrels of fish overboard. The big ship sailed off to the east of Carbery Island to pick up there, in a more sheltered situation. The Wills had a good whiskey when they got back into Canty's, where a supply was always kept!

> Timothy O'Mahony from Goleen was at Gurthdove pier to meet a ship that was to take some barrels away. The ship arrived but there was a strike on board in the ship's hold. O'Mahony asked if Joseph Downey and Dick Daly would stow the barrels on board the ship. They said that they would and off they set. The two men had only shifted a couple when one of the ship's crew let loose an iron bar onto Dick, and knocked him out, cold. Dick went blue and Joseph was a-feared for his life, so he called down to the lads in the faller to help get Dick back onto dry land, and eventually they got him up onto the pier. Timothy O'Mahony got his brandy out and they tried him with that. After a time, one man said that it was a pity to waste good brandy on a dead man. O'Mahony sent for his son who was a priest. He arrived and a pile of prayers were said over Dick. After a good while he came around. The ship's crew loaded the rest of the barrels without question and Timothy O'Mahony wrote off to the Limerick Steam Ship Co., on behalf of Dick Daly, who received £28 as compensation.

After the season's fishing all the nets were barked in a ceiler (a flat bottomed iron pot) at Dunmanus or Goleen, but later the Timmys had one. The ceiler would be full of boiling water and bark (a non-sticky type of tar), and the nets were steeped for a good spell. Barking drove out the salt and would preserve the cotton mesh for the next year's fishing. The nets, when being repaired, were spread out in a field. In Dunkelly the field was called the Seine Field, and at Gurthdove it was at Willie's Paircnafarriga. Only the experienced and older men were allowed to repair the nets, as the younger lads rarely had enough care for a job that had to be done so well.

A sad end for a seine boat

Although the barrels of fish were taken throughout the season by the fish buyers, it was on November Dark that the seine crews received their money. The fish buyers were Timothy O'Mahony, Jer Sheehan from Kilbrown, and later, Flynn, Mike Sweeny (agent for MacKenna from Dingle) and John Dwyer of Baltimore, who stayed with Ellie Collins in Dunkelly. One of the fish buyers brought his own whiskey to Canty's one day. He had it in his sidecar. The men found it and they drank the lot! The price of the fish varied according to how scarce they were. In the nineteen-twenties the price could be from 3/- to 15/- per long hundred (132 fish). The money from the sale of the fish was made into shares; one share for each of the twelve men, two for the seine boat, and one for the

Remains of seining gear

faller boat, making a total of 15 shares. There was always a grand ball after the fish buyers had paid up, with plenty of dancing, drink and baccy. The ball lasted until the dawn of day. Often it was also a farewell night to those who were going overseas. At the height of seining sixty men went out from Canty's Cove with five seines, four owned by Dunkelly men and one seine from Ballydevlin. Gurthdove and Toor had one seine each and Dunmanus had four seines. With the arrival of the Second World War in 1939, Jer Sheehan sold the last 300 barrels of mackerel from Canty's Cove. Ricky Paul's seine carried on for a few years after that, but by the mid-forties seining on the Northside finished altogether. In 1949 Rick Allan walked to Balteen to John Rick (Collins) who had a share in a seine net. They agreed to sell it for twenty pounds to a man in Glengariff, but it was mighty hard parting with the past.

Emigration

Since the days of the Great Hunger, emigration, mostly to America but also to England or other countries, has been the cause of a steady decline in the population of the Northside, as in most parts of Ireland. William McCarthy went to Western Virginia after the famine, but later returned. His son, also William McCarthy, went to the oil fields in America but returned to farm and fish in Dunkelly Middle. In the first quarter of this century, five of his seven children went to America but only Jim and Tom came back.

With big families in those days, there wasn't enough food and work to go round, and when a young member of the family emigrated, it usually meant that they would never see 'home' again. Their tragic departures are well recorded in 'Green Goleen', 'Sailing for Americay, 'Parish of Sweet Kilmoe' and other poems. Every family on the Northside had relations, sometimes going back three generations, that emigrated to America. Many of the young boys and girls had some relative in the place that they were bound for, who would help them in their huge adjustments to their new way of life. The families who were left behind often had a rosy view of emigration, but it was hard and bitter for the young boys and girls who

Some of the McCarthy (Wills) family of Dunkelly Middle. c. 1910

departed. Mickeen Pairca, from the Poundland, would crochet gifts of ties and scarves for people who emigrated, as a token from the Northside. In the mid nineteen-twenties, twenty-eight people left the Northside. Another big draft of people went after the finishing of seining, in 1939.

When someone was emigrating there was always a gathering of friends and neighbours on the eve of the day of departure. There would be drink, tobacco, songs and talk until the dawn of day, when they would strike out for Cork.

> My name is Muesheen Durkin
> And I'm sick and tired of working,
> No more I'll pick the praties,
> No longer I'll be poor,
> For as sure as my name is Kearney!
> I'm off to California!
> Where, instead of picking praties
> I'll be digging lumps of gold!

ONLY FOUR GUINEAS!!!

FROM QUEENSTOWN TO NEW YORK
On WEDNESDAY next, 10th AUGUST,

THE Splendid First-class swift screw steam-ship

"KEDAR,"

Of the celebrated "CUNARD COMPANY'S Line.
FARE, with full Diet and unequalled Accommodation;

Reduced to £4 4s. 0d.!!!
D. M. HENNESSY,
Denton House, Tralee,

August 3rd, 1864.   Agent.

Queenstown (Cobh, Cork)

GReeɲ Goleeɲ

It was in the month of April in the year of '64,
I Left my native country and friends to see no more.
They escorted me to Skibbereen where a train for me was due,
I stepped on and the train sped off, to green Goleen I bid my last adieu.

We passed along through various towns, as to Cork we were bound.
We admired the scenes so beautiful, and the country side as we passed through.
We admired the River Lee, where ships sped up and down,
But I cannot compare it to green Goleen where I bid my last adieu.

We stayed that night at Mackey's hotel, a dozen of us and more,
We danced and sang the whole night long, as we did the night before.
But at seven o'clock in the morning, the tender for me was due,
I stepped on, and it sped off, to green Erin I bid my last adieu.

Now I'm in Americay and settled down for life,
I'll write home to my parents and friends, who I left behind.
Here's to dear old Queenstown that lovely spot to view
But I can not compare it to green Goleen where I bid my last adieu.

Queenstown quay

Sailing for Americay

Now sons and son's daughters of Erin's green isle,
Have patience a moment and listen awhile.
Our sons and son's daughters are all gone away,
And thousands are sailing for Americay.

The night before leaving they met the neighbours and boys,
Early next morning their heart's gave great sighs.
They kiss their fond mothers and daughters and say,
"Good bye darling parents, we're going faraway."

Their friends and their daughters and neighbours also
Their trunk it is packed and is ready to go,
The tears from their eyes they fall down like the rain,
When the horses are starting off north for the train.

When you reach the station you can hear the last cry,
With handkerchiefs waving and bidding good bye.
Their parents will tell them be sure and to write
And always to think of those far out of sight.

Well, they launch the steamer after leaving the strand,
They give one last look at their own native land,
Each heart it will break on leaving their shore,
Good bye to old Ireland, we will ne'er see it no more.

Good luck to those people and safe may they land,
They're leaving their home for a far distant strand,
Here in old Ireland our land will turn stale,
As thousands are sailing for Americay.

The Parish of Sweet Kilmoe

Farewell my dearest Mary, to Americae I must make my way
And its many a pleasant evening together we did stray.
It grieves my heart to have to part and bid a long adieu,
To friends so kind I left behind in the Parish of Sweet Kilmoe.

Sad and lonely was the hour when we were forced to part,
With parents dear and comrade boys and the fond ones of my heart.
In a foreign strand I mean to land for my fortune to pursue
But the scenes behind I will bear in mind, the Parish of Sweet Kilmoe.

It's at many a fair in sweet Goleen that I spent a happy day
In dancing and in singing the time we did pass away.
The flowing glass around we passed for our spirits to renew.
I will ne'er forget those happy days in the Parish of Sweet Kilmoe.

It was from Queenstown Harbour our good ship did set sail
With cheerful boys and girls from poor old Gránawaile.
Who were forced to leave their dear old homes for a new one to pursue,
Sure I thought that day our hearts 'twould break, for home in Sweet Kilmoe.

When I reach Columbus's shore where freedom all is mine,
I will never forget those happy days I spent in Erin's Isle,
Where in childhood days I wandered and troubles were but few,
I will ne'er forget, though faraway, the Parish of Sweet Kilmoe.

So now I'm in a foreign land, strange faces there I do see
But none so dear and kind to my heart as those of Carbery.
Although I have travelled across the sea to them I will be true,
The neighbours kind I have left behind in the Parish of Sweet Kilmoe.

Now to finish up and make an end and I hope to see some day,
My parents dear and comrade boys, once more to sport and play.
And my own colleen, with a smile serene and a heart that was always true,
To roam the paths and the green hillsides of the Parish of Sweet Kilmoe.

Some of the men of Dunkelly regularly went to Scotland to work on the late harvest there, but they were always back in time to give the woman of the house the money for 'bringing in the Christmas'. Other bachelor men went to England, but would not come back until the beginning of the farming year in February.

Other employment

The traders of Goleen, O'Mahony, Scully, Barnett and Camier, would employ the people from the Northside to unload the boats in Goleen. If the boat was not unloaded at the slack of high water you would have to wait for the next high water, and the store owner would have to pay for the waiting boat. One time O'Mahony got some other people to unload a boat but he was caught up with the tide, and so he had to pay extra for the boat laying idle. The next time he went back for the Northside men, Timothy O'Mahony said that he, "Never knew that there was so much power in the tail of the little mackerel!" Many of the boats that ran from Cork City to Goleen were owned and captained by Capers (people from Cape Clear). Northsiders were employed for unloading the boats until the arrival of good roads and lorries.

The Dhurode copper mine was first officially opened in 1843 'by Consolidated and West Carbery Mining Company' (probably started by the Reverend Trail of Schull and Captain Foster). For three years 229 tons of copper ore were sold, raising a total of £629. There were no figures for 1847 and this may well have been due to the famine and the fact that there was no one able to work. In 1850 'the Mining Company of Ireland' spent £800 on a survey, and decided that it was not worth mining. From that time onwards Dhurode fell into ill repute. In 1852 to 1856 a 'Bubble Company' called the 'Dhurode Copper Mining Company' raised £20,000 in London. It mined 24 tons with an ore value of £156! Dividends were paid out at four shillings and four pence, which gave a sum of over four-thousand pounds, thirty times the value of the ore that had been mined! Gold was discovered at Lackavawn. A stamp was installed at Dhurode which could process 150 to 200 tons of copper and gold ore a month. The stamp did not work as there was not enough water pressure, or gold! Cheques started to bounce and the mining captain, Charles Thomas, was sacked but refused to leave until £26-9-11 was paid to him. The 'Dhurode Copper Mining Company' collapsed in 1858. Someone was getting rich, but it wasn't the Northsiders! The 'South West Ireland Mining Company' set up and said that they were opening a smelter at Dhurode. Two-thousand shares at £2-10-0 were offered and William Tompkin made £50 a month as Mining Captain. In 1859 fourteen tons of ore was sold for £73, but there was no smelting. The 'South West Ireland Mining

Company' closed and yet another company (unknown) was set up! In 1862 the 'Dhurode Copper and Lead Mining Company' was formed to raise shares on the London stock exchange, but people were learning and it didn't raise any capital. In the eighteen-seventies Lord Bandon was offering local people 3/- a ton for iron and manganese ore. No big

The powder magasine at Dhurode. 1986

deposits were ever found. In 1881 the 'Atlantic Mining Company Ltd' ran tests there over two years, but to no avail. From 1900 to 1906 the 'Dhurode Copper Company' officially mined one ton of ore from Dhurode, Lackavawn and Dunmanus West. It was said that a good deal more than that was taken out to the ships!

A few stories are remembered about mining at Dhurode. It was hard, cramped and unpleasant work and not many cared for it. The people from Balteen worked at Dhurode as well as the Coughlans (Kits) of Lackavawn, the Downeys of Gurthdove and the Donovans of Dunkelly, but the rest of the crowd preferred the sea to that kind of work.

Around the time of the great hunger, a group of men were down in the mine shaft at Dhurode, when a whole pile of them passed out. Those that hadn't, managed to get the others back up out of the mine. After a time the men all came round. The Captain of the mine was Charles Thomas, who was a decent sort of a man. He was concerned as to why some of the men passed out, and not others, with the gas and fumes. He enquired as to what they had for breakfast. All the men who passed out said that they had had only cake and water, whereas, the men that were fine down below, had cake, milk and butter. The captain gave the poor, hungry men a bit to eat, and said that they had to have a good feed before working down the mine.

At the turn of the century, John Coughlan (Johnny Kit) and four others working at Dhurode, were sent away for slats (long thin stones). They found a few slats but one of the stones that they met was half under the ground, so they prised it up onto its edge and the stone started to trickle blood. They let the slat back down as they said that somebody might be buried there. They hadn't brought back enough stone, so Johnny and his team went out again with the Captain of the mine and it wasn't long before they met the same stone. Johnny explained what had happened before, and Captain Worseldine said that if he himself had been sent to fetch it he would have brought it, but if they felt that way they should leave it. And so they did.

Dhurode Mine

Dhurode's hill and valley is the fairest to be behold,
There are sparkling gems of silver bright and lumps of copper ore,
Now that valley's fine machinery it's equal cannot be found,
'Twas erected by McCormick's from the heart of Goleen town.

They drained that lovely valley, they put the water up and down,
They formed a great hydraulic for to turn the big wheel around,
There are stone crushers, water wheels and the finest machinery,
It is all in charge of old Pad Long and owned by an English company.

At the first revolution that the big wheel made the pumps began to flow
"Agabagaboy!" cried old Pad Long "I see tons of copper ore,
Now boys hold to the cable and keep the drive well straight,
B'gorra, we'll put the water whistling down Dunmanus Bay."

Now should you enter that fine valley on a dark and dreary night,
You'd think it 'twas a big city all lit with the electric light,
Travel this wide world, oe'r and oe'r and no happier boys you'd see,
Than Dan Reilly and Con Coughlan and the three sons of Big Curley.

From 1906 onwards Dhurode mine fell silent, and was left to the rabbits, the turf cutters and the poteen makers.

One day Poteen was being distributed in Dunkelly. Two lads from Gurthdove were coming home from Goleen when they passed two gardai. The lads knew what was on and so went full steam ahead to their homes and sent a couple of other's to warn the people of Dunkelly. The gardai arrived at Dunkelly to find nothing but were suspicious of the two boys that they had met on the road earlier, so they thought that they would check them out. The two lads from Gurthdove were found at their homes, sitting down to a meal. And that was the end of the matter.

One night William McCarthy heard a pony and trap on the road. It was late in the night and Will thought that it might be the gardai making their way to raid the poteen brewers at Dhurode so he quickly saddled the horse and off he went. The gardai stopped him, by Allans Corner, and asked where was he heading for. Will the Hare explained that his wife was having a baby so he was going to get a midwife and that if the gardai wouldn't let him through, he would hold them responsible. With that the gardai let Will through and he went like the wind to Dhurode, to pass on the news to the poteen brewers. To avoid the oncoming gardai on his way home, he went the long way around. Will the Hare was treated well for his good deed.

There was a time, when on a Sunday, drink was prohibited unless you were a traveller or lived more than three miles from town. Neddy Hodnett was living at Coslows at the time and he went into a bar with a friend at Goleen. The gardai raided the bar and questioned Neddy who said that he lived more than three miles from town. The matter didn't rest, and Neddy insisted that the gardai measured the road. The chain was got and the measuring began. It was under three miles to the front door. The pressure was on Neddy so he told the gardai that he had come out the back door. The gardai asked why he hadn't used the front door to which Neddy replied that there was a child in a cradle blocking the way. Measurements to the back door were made, and it was found to be just over three miles. By a hair's breath Neddy won the day!

Northsiders also worked at the 'Brow Head Quarry', which was opened by the Rowe Brothers of Liverpool, in 1925, at Castlemehigan (opposite Crookhaven). It was dirty and unhealthy work, and the men were covered in a fine dust from the crusher that made the small chips for the roads. The rock went out to the ships hold on a conveyor belt. The quarry employed one hundred people to start with but then the number went down to thirty-nine, and with the out break of The Second World War, it closed.

The Lobster Pond opened in 1926 and provided employment in boxing up the lobsters. For the fishermen there was a new boom in

'Brow Head Quary' from Crookhaven

lobsters and crawfish. The Pond halted for a time during the Second World War but finally closed down, in 1977.

From the outbreak of the Second World War employment was scarce. The Board of Works introduced the road improvement scheme, as a means of employment. The dole at that time was three shillings a week, whereas working on the roads paid six shillings a day. Single men worked four days a week for £1-4-0, and married men worked five days for £1-10-0. Some 22 men from the Northside worked on the roads and piers in Lackavawn, Gurthdove and Dunkelly. The Gangers were Bobby Allan, Patrick Cunningham and Christopher O'Sullivan. Making ends meet was hard from 1939 through to the nineteen-seventies, until Ireland joined the Common Market.

In 1965 the Barley Cove Hotel was built and it gave a great lift to the area. Northside men worked on its construction and ever since women have worked there, too.

The Hotel Song

Nineteen sixty-five was the date of the year,
The time for the Hotel was now drawing near,
The work it had started and all things going well,
When the rich men in Goleen began for to swell.

They wrote to Board Failte for to turn it down,
They wanted the tourists to leave their money in town.
But now that the project is well under way,
Ten chalets will be ready for the tenth day of May.

To accommodate tourists from over the sea
They'll make a nice place out of old Canawee,
There are skilled men and labourers from all parts around,
And their boss is a Cork man, his likes can't be found.

They're paying big wages. I heard people say,
So our boys and our girls at home now can stay.
When the summer was over they then closed it down
And started more work for our men all around.

To improve the Hotel and make it look grand,
With a fine tennis court made below in the strand,
And then when they started they wanted some stone
To lay more foundations and add to the road.

They were sent to Dhurode by a man I won't say,
But Tim Sheehan came along and he drove them away,
But now they have settled, and Tim got his pay,
The lorries are drawing without any delay.

When 'tis finished I'm sure 'twill look swell,
With twenty-two chalets around the Hotel,
And now when the tourists will come into Cork
They can go out to the Hotel, 'tis next to New York!

They'll have plenty of fine music and all kinds of fun,
And a fine sunny strand for to stretch in the sun.

December

Gloria in excelsis Deo
et in terra pax
hominibus, bonae voluntatis.

The long black nights, and the dark, bare rocks of the hillsides were brightened by preparations and 'bringing in' the family Christmas, to celebrate the birth of Christ. There was plenty of fun and games too, on Wren Day. With the old year dead and gone, it was time for the New Year to unfold.

The Turkey Buying Song

You all know Paddy Sheehan he is a businessman in Kilbrown
And when the turkey market came he thought of a good plan
He then hired Paddy Courcey from a land called Lackavawn
And they didn't leave one turkey from here to Kilcrohane.

When they got back to Durrus it was six o'clock at night,
They struck for Clonakilty for the turkeys would get light,
They put them in the market where they received their pay
They then went to Fahy's and got themselves some tea.

And turning home that very night and everything going well,
They picked up some of the turkeys they left with Din John L
That was engaged by customers, I heard the people say,
For the turkey, he is all the go for dinner on Christmas Day.

When they came back to Goleen 'twas near to closing time
They then went into Coughlans where they took a gin and lime
Paddy Sheehan took out his book I'm telling you no lie
He wrote a cheque for £2.10 and gave it to his boy.

So now to conclude and finish I have no more to say
But Paddy Sheehan was telling me Muintir Bháire takes the sway,
For rising heavy turkeys their likes aren't to be found,
For some of the turkey pushers there went as high as forty pound.

Christmas

With Christmas on it's way the women went into Goleen to 'bring in the Christmas' from the shops. Each of the stores would give a Christmas Box that befitted your custom, and children would be given a penny for sweets. There was always a good supply of poteen from Dhurode for the occasion. The house and farm were tidied up and put into good order.

A RAFFLE № 1775

AT GOLEEN HALL,

ON TUESDAY 8TH DECEMBER, 1953
(In aid of Goleen Parish Fund)

1st Prize	-	Raleigh Bicycle (Ladies' or Gent's)
2nd Prize	- - - -	£3
3rd Prize	- - -	£2

TICKETS 6d Each   (Book of 11 Tickets 5/-)

For Holy Year in 1950, a cross was placed on the top of Knocnaphuca. The materials for it were taken to the Scullys and from there up as far as possible by Jerome's horse and car. After that a donkey with a back-load was used, but for the last pull to the top of Knocnaphuca the materials had to go by manpower. For a number of Christmases afterwards the cross was lit up. In 1968 the cross was struck by lightning and that was the end of it.

Christmas Eve was a day of fast until the family evening meal. On this day the kitchen window, the holy pictures, the dresser and the clevy were decorated with holly and ivy by the children. There were mischievous little people on each of the points of the holly and if you played with them, you'd get a sharp pinch! Before the evening meal the kitchen window in the house would have a large candle, often red, placed in it and, with a prayer from the man of the house, the youngest lit it, to welcome Joseph and Mary. After the lighting of the candle it was time for the evening meal of fish, the best being ling, or sometimes hake, with white sauce and potatoes. After that, the man would stretch himself out on the settle, whilst the woman of the house set the fire a-blazing by

The Christmas candle

turning the wheel of the fire machine, and sweets and apples were given to the children. The cattle got an extra good feed for the night, along with plenty of bedding. It was said to be unlucky to be still awake at midnight, and so it was early to bed for all.

The family got out of bed well before the cock crowed, as Mass on Christmas Day was held at seven in the morning. The children had to see inside their stocking that had been pinned to the clevy for Santa to fill. The woman of the house would start to get the feast ready for mid-day, and the man of the house would get the donkey and car tackled up. After Mass it was straight home. It was strictly a family day and not for visitors unless asked. The presents were only small offerings, on account of times being hard, but they were always well received and with much excitement. A young cock or goose with the corned (salted) bacon from November, was traditional fair on Christmas Day. With full bellies and a good heat from the fire, any letters or cards from America or overseas would be read out, along with general chat and merriment.

Wren Day

On Christmas Eve the lads had to kill a wren in preparation for their outing on Wren Day (St Stephen's Day, 26th December). It could be many hours before a wren was killed, and sometimes they had to go out after the mid-day meal on Christmas Day before one was caught. The usual way to catch a bird was to use a special basket made for the purpose. The basket was pyramid shaped with four sides. The bait was a small handful of corn placed under the basket that was propped up on one side with a cipín (a small stick). A bow made of twig was set as the spring that knocked the cipín out of place when a bird landed on it, and the basket went down. The other way to take a

A happy Christmas for – ALL!

bird was to prop up a heavy slat (long thin rock) with a stick, which was attached to a length of sugán rope. With the corn bait in place you waited for the bird, and with the taut rope you pulled the stick out and the slat went down. Up to the late nineteen-sixties, at different times of the year according to the nesting season rock pigeons, blackbirds, thrushes, golden plover and snipe would be caught and eaten.

For the wren it was different. It was bad luck to kill a wren at any time of the year other than at Christmas. The lads tore up and down the ditches and in and out of fuchsia, furze and briar looking for their bird.

Wren Day was a special day, especially for the lads. The wren was pinned with holly and ribbons, to a pole of about five foot. The Wren Boys would dirty their faces and dress up in home made skirts and wigs of straw, before setting out to visit houses, where they sang their 'Wren Day Song' to receive food, drink or a few pennies. Other areas had Wren Boys, but it was the first faction of Wren Boys who called to a house that would get the prize; however you were always guaranteed a good reception in your own townland. With the awakening of the sun, so as to get a good pull out of other areas, the Wren Boys made their way west to Balteen and Toor, across south, to Letter, east to Goleen, and then back to the Northside. A cow's horn would be blown at every chance but more recently a brass lorry horn was used. Every house was stopped at, and if there wasn't a reply, the Wren Pole was repeatedly tapped on the upper

The Wren Day Song (Northside version)

The wren, the wren, the king of all the birds,
On St. Stephen's day she was caught on the furze,
Although she is little her family is great.
Rise up landlady and fill us a treat.

What far la, la la de, What far la, la la de.

We hunted our wren three miles and more
From Dunmanus Castle to Lackavawn,
Through ditches and hedges and fields so green
The devil of sport was ever yet seen.

As we were going up through Canawee
We spied our wren up on top of a tree,
Up with our cupid[1] and broke her knee
And we brought her to our holly tree.

Our wren is here quite plain to be seen,
She is mounted high on our holly tree.
A bunch of ribbons by her side
With the Northside boys to be her guide.

Last Saturday night I was cooking the plum[2]
When I burned my hand and I do feel it numb,
Between my finger and my thumb,
And a blister rose as big as a plum!

If you fill us of the best
We hope in heaven your soul will rest,
If you fill us of the small
It won't agree with our boys at all.

So to Mr . . . [3], my worthy man,
It is to your house we brought our wren,
Not for the sake of money or beer,
But to wish you a merry Christmas and a happy New Year.

My box it do shake and it makes a great rattle,
So down with the pan and up with the kettle,
Give us your answer and let us be gone!

[1] Bow.
[2] Christmas plum pudding.
[3] The name of the householder.

windows until the door was opened, whereupon the Wren Boys would sing their song, waiting for an offering from the house. If different factions of Wren Boys should meet there was often fighting. They would plunder from one another the day's hard earnings.

The music makers. Paul Sheehan (electrician) and Tommy Hodnett (postman). 1994

In 1976 the Wren Boys used Tommy Hodnett's van as the mode of transport. The people in the parish of Goleen thought that this was not the same as doing it on foot and so the Wren Boys went further afield, starting in Bandon and ending up in Durrus or Schull! 1983 saw the last of the Wren Boys from the Northside.

The Wren Ball was a great event, and it was held as close as possible to St. Stephen's Day, as on the day itself the Wren Boys would be exhausted from the day's efforts. Danny Donovan's was the usual house on the Northside for the ball. The Wren Boys' booty went towards the porter, sweetcake and baccy. The men would also pay an entry fee for the night, to cover any remaining costs. A grand time was had by all with the ball finishing with the dawn of day.

Death and Wakes

Anyone who died in the Twelve Days of Christmas or on a Friday and be buried on the Sunday would go straight to heaven and it was a sure way to get a grand send off! 'A green Christmas would bring a red graveyard.' If Christmas was mild it meant that there was a long, hard slog of winter ahead and a good few deaths. With a death in the family, besides the bereavement, there was the cost of the coffin and burial, which, in those times, was very hard to find.

> When people died from different families, different signs would be seen or heard beforehand. The McCarthys had a blue light that would follow the family. The Coughlans of Lackavawn and the Flors in the Poundland had the Banshee that was heard on several different occasions. When Bridie McCarthy died in 1938, Pad the Rock heard the sound of timber planks being dropped the night before.

> In August 1963 Dan Coughlan of Gurthdove (a lighthouse keeper) went to see Pad the Rock at Bantry hospital. The nurse said he was fine and that Pad would be home by the weekend, and that Dan could go back to work. Dan struck out for the Northside and he was at Cnonacán of a Road when he saw a blue light going from cock to cock. Dan knew that there wasn't much time left for Pad. He

arrived back home and told everyone that the nurse at the hospital said that Pad would be fine, but he had seen the blue light in the field. Pad the Rock died a couple of days after.

Jerry Paty saw a light, that went south-east at the rock above the house, on the night that his brother died in America. It was nearly a week before the telegram arrived with the sad news.

As soon as someone died, the clock, if there was one, was stopped and a piece of furniture and two chairs were placed upside down outside the front door, to keep the little people from taking the dead person's soul. There was always a friend of the family in the house, which was never locked, even for the removal and burial. If the person died after midnight, the neighbours and friends would go to the wake for that night and the next day and night. The wake on the Northside was as for the whole of the Parish of Kilmoe. It was not the same as other areas of Ireland where it could be of an unruly nature, but, nevertheless there was always plenty of porter, tobacco and talk of who was related or had a call to whom. It was considered that if you were anything more than a fourth cousin that you were a distant relative, but you would have a call to the family. You could almost always find a call to any family on the Northside, or in the Parish of Kilmoe. The best way to show sympathy towards the bereaved family would be to prove kinship, and with each link between your family and theirs, there would be a story about that relative, their land or some recitation that they told, until you reached the dead person themselves. On some occasions other stories were told, but there was never any dancing, games or songs. There was always high respect for the family and for the dead.

The Rosary was said towards midnight and it started off slow and steady but would gradually pick up in speed until you didn't know what was said, when. It was only the experienced who could respond, and with a thunder of speech the incantation was complete. The weight of people made their way home, but the relations and close neighbours stayed until day break.

A woman on the Northside had an old relation who died in the house. The old lady was waked, the Rosary was said and the most of the people had gone home. The woman was tired and so went up to sleep a-while on her bed. After a time two lads came to pray over the body. The young people downstairs sent them up to the woman's bedroom and not to the room below where the old lady was. There came an almighty commotion from up above, the woman woke with a fright to the sound of prayers and two lads praying over her! They tore out of the room and down stairs, as they thought that the corpse had come alive again!

The Removal and Burial

Shortly before a removal, two priests would come to say prayers over the dead person. The body was always left in the room that they died in and if they had been ill for some time their sick bed would have been placed in the parlour on the ground floor, so as to make it easy for nursing. The men folk of the house would put the corpse into the coffin and then pass around a noggin of whiskey. If the person died upstairs, sometimes a window had to be taken out, on account that the stairs were too tight to get the coffin down in a respectable manner. This was done by threading a rope through the handles and then letting it down a ladder placed at the window. Two chairs were turned upright and the coffin was placed on them for a minute. From there it was put on the side car, and the two chairs turned upside down again and left until after the burial. Willie Goggin made many of the coffins for the Northside and Timothy Collins (senior) had a smart side-car, that was used for the removal and there was always a woman, wearing a shawl, to caoin by his side.

The Mareens, at the foot of Knocnaphuca, is a lonesome place. There are three separate accounts of the same strange happening there. On the first recorded occasion a priest was involved. With the other two occasions, different men reported that it was as if they were in the middle of a removal, and that there was a great darkness and pressure upon them.

One night a man had to get the priest, Father Daniel O'Connell, from Goleen as his wife was very ill. They came back over to the Northside and he gave the woman the last rights. Father O'Connell was always lonesome at night time, and he asked if the man would go with him back to Goleen. They set off and had reached Géaracnoc, past the Turn of Curly Shea on Knocnaphuca, when Father O'Connell asked the man did he see anything? To which the man replied that he had not. They stepped on a-piece, and once again he asked the

Father D. O'Connell's grave

man did he see anything? The reply came, that he had not. Father O'Connell asked the man to come around to his other side, which the man did, and he asked, what did he see now? The man replied that he saw the hill black with people, as many as there were blades of grass in a field. Father O'Connell told the man to keep close and follow him on his journey. They both arrived back at the priest's house, and when Father O'Connell had dismounted he asked if the

man would be lonesome to go back home. The man said that he would, so Father O'Connell blessed him and told him to go back home, and that he would not see or hear a thing until he arrived back at home.

Father Daniel O'Connell helped people in need in many ways, but especially with cures of the mind and depressions, and he was buried at St. Patrick's Churchyard Goleen in 1879. Even after his death people made rounds to his grave and left ribbons, Rosaries and other offerings.

The burial ground for the Northside used to be at either Kilmoe or Cill Cheangail. At the Poundland, in Dunkelly Middle, was the Killeenagh burial ground for non-baptised children. In the times of the Great Hunger, Killeenagh as well as Kilmoe and Cill Cheangail were used for burials. In more recent times many have been taken to Goleen, although Kilmoe is still the traditional burial ground for the Northside.

In the eighteen-eighties there was a boy from Balteen by the name of O'Sullivan. One evening he went looking for a goat that had strayed. The boy found himself in the Kilmoe Burial Ground and the night caught him, so he decided to sleep in the ruins of Kilmoe Church. He was woken in the night by a priest calling for someone to answer Mass. The boy said that he would. The priest replied that he had been waiting 100 years, and that he could not get anyone to answer. The Mass was said and the O'Sullivan boy went back to sleep, and in the morning he found his goat, and went home happy. A priest who died without saying a Mass that he had promised to someone would not rest until he had the Mass said.

Kilmoe Church

The Old Lady

In olden days there was a man and wife, who like many, were very poor. They had one cow, that in the end, they had to sell. The man went away to the fair, wherever the fair was held. He was just going into the village when he came across a sergeant and two policemen who were just after arresting a man and were taking him to the barracks. "What has the poor man done?" asked your man. "None of your business," replied the sergeant. "Oh," said the man, "it is a shame to see a man being arrested so early in the morning." "Well," said the sergeant, "if you give me the cow, you can have the man." The deal was struck.

Your man went back home with the other man but with ne'er a bit to eat for all the children. After a while the woman of the house asked your man how much did he get for the cow? He told her his story. "That was all right," said the woman, "but we don't have a bit to eat." "Is that so?" said the rescued man. "It was," they said. The night came upon them and the man asked did anyone around have any praties in the area and that they would go and get some. "Oh, no!" said the man of the house, 'I can't do anything like that!" "Give me a sack or two." said the man. He went out and that night he collected three bags of praties. "Now you're not too bad," he said to the family.

The next night he asked if there were any sheep around. There were. He asked the man would he come along. "Oh, no!" said the man, "I would never do a thing like that!" Your man went out, and killed three sheep. There was plenty of meat for all. "Now you're not too bad," he said.

This man was a man of learning who had books. He also had on him a long black coat like a clergy man. He used to walk out on the road and read a lot. Of course the potatoes and sheep were missing but they all said he was some kind of monk or blessed man and that he wouldn't do anything like that.

One fine day he had rambled a long ways away. He came to a very rich house belonging to a Protestant landlord. He asked for something to eat. They said come in and were very good to him. The owner's mother was dying and there was a Protestant minister with her. Through the door your man heard that she wouldn't be happy lest she be buried with seven dresses on her and five hundred sovereigns put in a box by her head in the coffin, when she died. Your man took it in and went back home to the man and wife. A week later the old lady of the big house died. She was taken to the graveyard, buried and prayed on.

That night your man said, "Come with me, for the old woman has seven dresses on and five hundred sovereigns by her head." "Oh, no!" said the man of the house, "I would never do a thing like that." Your man then tried the wife. "I will," she said, and off they went with spade and sack.

They took the seven dresses and one hundred sovereigns, for that was all that was put there. Your man sent the wife home. He got a rope and put the corpse up on his back and took her back to where she left. He found the milk house. He gave great upset to the place, he splattered up and around the walls and ceiling the milk from the pans and the cream from the tubs. There was one big barrel of cream next to which he placed the old lady, with her arm in the cream. He shut the door after him. He went away. The next day the big house awoke. They milked the cows, had breakfast and then went to the milk house. There came a roaring! The old lady had the whole place upset and her with all here dresses gone! They sent for a different clergyman. It was decided to bury her with ten dresses and six hundred sovereigns. This they did, and gave all day to praying over her.

The night came. Your man went to the wife and asked if she would go with him. She said that she would. They went, and they dug the old lady up again. He gave the wife the ten dresses and the six hundred sovereigns and told her to go home. He took the old lady to the big house once again, only this time he propped her up against the front door with a twig to keep her steady. The big house awoke with a roar, screams and shouting. The clergyman said that he could do no more. One wise man suggested that they might send for this travelling holy man and that he might know a bit about something. They did. Your man said that he didn't know, and that there was something very wrong all right, but to try twelve dresses on her and one thousand sovereigns by her head. "I also have a book here that I haven't read for over twenty years, which might, I'm not

saying that it will, but it might keep her away." "Well," said the landlord, "if you do, I'll keep you for the rest of your life."

The old lady was buried, prayers were said. That night, the travelling man and the man's wife dug her up again. They took the money and the dresses and put her back down again.

One week . . . Two weeks . . .

Three weeks went by and the old lady never came back. The landlord wanted the travelling man to stay with him. He said that he wouldn't and that he would stay with the man he was with. The landlord built a big house for them and they lived long and died happy.

That's my story for you, and with the help of God, I'll have another for you tomorrow night, sitting by the open fire.

Conclusion

Like the passing year, it was always said that when one person died another was born to replace them. The present and future Northsiders will bring their own customs and stories to the new millennium and, please God, remember those of the past with gratitude.

The stories in this book have been handed down orally, often when gathered around the warmth of a kitchen fire, a tradition which has changed little over the centuries until our technological age arrived. The old people who knew these stories and the way of life that went with them, are also fading away. John-J, a much loved companion of all who knew him, and especially the young people, died a year ago and another link with the past was broken.

As, on leaving an old and recently emptied house, the motes of dust are lit up by the warmth of the sun's last rays, to drift and settle, as you quietly shut the door for the last time, so we hope that we have illuminated many of the old ways of the Northside for you.

'By the word Amen is meant, so be it, and it be so, shut this book and let me go.'

Rath Dé ar na léitheorí go léir

John J. Coughlan, 1997

Glossary

The spelling of Gurthdove and Lackavawn, in the book, have been spelt in the way that the people who live there spell them. Other spellings for Gurthdove are; Gortdov, Gortdubh and Gortduff and the other spelling for Lackavawn is Lackavaun.

Agin	Against
Baccy	Tobacco
Back-loaders	Baskets for donkeys (creel) or for man (cisean)
Bairín breac	Fruit cake
Bán	White
Banshee	A spirit that foretells a death in a family
Barraois	Phosphorescence in the sea
Barrfhód	Top sods with heather root from the hills
Béillic	Cavern at the base of vertical rock face
Blast	Cow mastitis or a strong wind
Bloc	Anchor
Bórán	A sieve made from wood and hide for winnowing
Boistin	The first milk from a cow that has just calved
Bonham (banbh)	Piglet
Boreen	Small lane
Borhán	Dried cow pat or donkey / horse droppings for the fire
Breac	Rough ground in a field where furze grows
Brehóg	Flock of sheep
Briar	Bramble
Brone	Heat haze
Bucán	Foot rest of potato spade
Buchrillán Bhuide	Ragwort, *Senecio jacobaea*
Budarí	Northside slang for men from Muintia Bháire
Bullaun	Cupped rock
Bunce	Boundary
Caoin	Lament the dead
Carraigín Moss	Carraigeen Moss (edible seaweed)
Ceiler	A large, flat bottomed pan
Chamber	A small building with four dry stone walls for animals
Cipín	Small stick
Copóg	Dock plant
Ciseán	Basket
Clevy	Mantle shelf
Cóbach	Black headed gull or generally any gull

Colleen	Girl
Connor	Wrasse (species of fish)
Cos	Base or foot (of hay rick)
Crahog	Black pollock
Craic	Talk and fun
Cré	(the Creed). Northside - to enhance
Creabhour	Stye in the eye
Creamery	Milk processing plant
Creel	Back-loaders (basket) for donkeys
Criothán	Small potato used for animal feed
Cró	Animal shelter, one curving wall from a ditch or béillic
Croc	Pot
Crúibín	Hoof or trotter (cow, pig)
Crúibínach	Cow hoof rot
Cuas	Cove or inlet
Cuiltán	Montegue's Blenny (species of fish)
Ditch	A raised earth bank
Earthing	Throwing earth from the trench to the top of the ridge
Erin	Old name for Ireland
Faller	The smaller 'Follower' boat for seine fishing
Faraheen	A foot long plank with a handle like a broom
Fiocadán	Marsh or Black thistle, *Cirsium palustre*
Fionnán	Purple Moor Grass, *Molinia caerulea*
Firing	Fuel for the fire
Fornog	A cow not calving for two years in a row
Foxy	Ginger in colour
Friese	Thick, woollen cloth
Furze	Gorse
Gabhairin rua	Jack snipe
Gabhlóg	Stick with a 'V' at the end, used with a hook to cut furze
Gansey	Jumper
Gearnán	Large rectangular rock, four to ten inches thick
Gneeve	Land measurement, locally said to be the grass of four cows
Grafán	Hand tool for hacking the earth
Greaseadán	White thistle, *Cirsium vulgare*
Greasuc	Red fire embers
Green	Often used instead of 'grass'
Grua	Side of a ridge of potatoes
Garda	Police (or gard)
Haggard	Farmyard
Heave	Swell

Helmas	A strong wind in September
Het	Heather
Hob	Fire place
Huer	Master of the seine and captain of the seine boat
Linhay	An lean-to attached to the gable end of a house
Leaca	Slope of a hill
Lougheen	Pond or small lake
Lonesome	Afraid
Lúchair	Grass and rushes found on flat wet ground (curragh)
Madragaoth	A wind-dog or part of a rainbow
Meitheal	A group of neighbours and friends to help at harvest
Miabhán	Edible seaweed
Milliceen	A midge
Miniheens	Muirneach, Ammophila arenaria, Marram grass
Muintir Bháire	Sheep's Head peninsula
Múnluch	The green scum around the yard manure heap
Narry the Bog	Heron
Pattern	A gathering of people and a dance on Holy Days
Pike	Pitch fork
Piseóg	A charm to ward off evil spells
Pounders	Large strand pebbles
Pratie	Potato
Prash	Mussels used as ground bait or fertiliser
Púca	Mischievous sprite (Fairy)
Pœcán	Mound of barrfhóds
Raisting	Preparing ground for turnips
Radlóc	Group of cattle
Raucs	Clumps of floating seaweed
Ridge of Graf	The 'lazy bed' system of planting potatoes
Ríobún	Wheat and milk 'porridge'
Rod	Coppiced, Goat Willow
Rón	Seal
Rów	Rock in the sea that is exposed by the low tide
Scallóg	Off-cut remains of a potato
Scairavin na gró	(- gCuach) A sharp wind in May (the last of the winter)
School	Shoal (of fish)
Sciff	Flat round basket for potatoes
Scoriachting	Visiting friends and neighbours at night
Scuttle	Crevice in rocks
Scrape	Furrow made by a plough
Shagga	Black diver, cormorant or a shag

Sheannachie	Story teller
Sheegwee	Fairy wind or whirl wind
Sleán	Spade for cutting black turf
Sleabh	A rough, open area for grazing, not always necessarily on a mountain
Slocán	Edible seaweed
Spánach	Burnt furze stem
Sprouter	Potato with sprouting shoots
Steampai	Potato based 'pancake' (stampy)
Strand	Shore or beach of pebbles or sand
Stripper	A cow not calving for one year
Sugán	Rope made with Fionnán or straw
T'aint	It is not
Tarft	Thwart (seat on a boat)
Teascán	A measure
Tiel	[In step (dance)]
Tocht	Mattress
Townland	Divisions within a Parish boundary
Tráheenoc	Dolphin
Trashil	Door frame
Trupán	Edible seaweed
Turf	Peat
Twig	Coppiced, Osier willow
Wrack	Flotsam

Notes and credits

§ Transcribed from recordings made by Hannah O'Driscoll in 1968.
‡ Transcribed from recordings made by Richard Hawkes in 1974.
† Cork County Record Office, Schools Manuscripts.
Coll. Collection
Anon. Anonymous

Particular thanks to, Bridget McCarthy and John and Mary Hawkes for photographs, and objects that have been photographed throughout the book. Other photographs are by Richard Hawkes. Many thanks to Thelma Ede for the story Illustrations.

January
Song, 'Ever Green and Fair Dunmanus', Author Dan O'Mahony (Dan the Fiddler), Collected by Hannah O'Driscoll.
Story, 'Pactrick Downey, The Glavins and the Mermaid', told by Jerry McCarthy.
Story, 'The Horned Woman', Anon. † and told by Jerry McCarthy.

February
Photograph credit, Coll., Maggie Courcey, 'Paddy Courcey'.
Photograph credit, Coll., Wigham Collection via Bill Swanton taken for Esnor, 'Oswestry'.
Technical Info., on ships, 'Shipwrecks of the Irish Coast'. Edward Bourke, 1991.
Song, 'The Iberian', Anon. Text from Bridie Kennedy (Dunmanus East).
Song, 'The Memphis', Anon. Text from Tommy Hodnett.

March
Story, 'The Matchmakers and the Butter', Told by Jerry McCarthy.
Song, 'The Pride of Carbery', Anon. As sung by Christopher O'Sullivan.
Story, 'William Downey', Told by Jerry McCarthy.
Story, 'To find a Bride', Anon. As told by Jerry McCarthy, ‡.

April
Photograph credit, Coll., Eileen Scully, 'Jerome Scully and Tractor'.
Photograph credit, Pat Murphy and Dick Hill, 'Goleen Creamery'.
Photograph credit, Coll. Timmy and Mary O'Sullivan, 'Milk to creamery'.
Photograph credit, Johnathon Stafford, 'Wild Goats'.
Song, 'The Tax Song', Anon. As sung by Dennis McCarthy, §.

May
Photograph credit, Coll., Michael Coughlan, 'Goleen'.
Photograph credit, Coll., Jimmy Downey, 'Nan O'Donovan and goose'.
Photograph credit, Coll., Finbar Coughlan, 'Goleen'.
Story, 'The Three Brothers', Anon. As told by Jerry McCarthy, ‡.

June
Photograph credit, Coll., Ellen Sullivan Sylvarns, 'Ellie Collins'.
Photograph credit, Coll., Timmy and Mary O'Sullivan, (Corran More), Turf cutters at Dhurode.
Song, 'The Bold Three Castles Head', Anon. Sung by Tom Barry (Cnoc, Lowertown).
Story, 'The Lazy Beauty and the Faries', Anon., †, and told by Jerry McCarthy.

July
Photograph credit, Coll., Julia Hodnett, 'The Hodnett Hay Rick'.
Photograph credit, Coll., Lawrence and Angela Stafford, 'Jerry Collins'.
Photograph credit, Coll., Jimmy Downey, 'O'Sullivan boat yard'.
Photograph credit, Coll., Bettie O'Leary, 'The Potato Crop'.
Story, 'The Farmer and the Woman', Anon. As told by Jerry McCarthy.
Story, 'The Cripples Leap', Anon., †.

August
Song, 'The Raid on Lackavawn', Anon. As sung by 'Sunny' Paul Sheehan (Cloghanaculleen).
Photograph credit, Owen Rich, 'Jerry Patty'.
Illustration, 'The Seine Boat', Seine Boat & Seine Fishing, 1990's, Allihies Folklore Group, illustration by Ruth Garside.
Song, 'Drowning in Dunmanus Bay', Anon., Bridie Kennedy (Dunmanus East).
Song, 'A Local Seine Boat Song', Anon. As sung by Peter Sheehan (Balteen). Recorded by Mary O'Driscoll in 1980's.
Photograph credit, Coll., Tess Cullinane, Photographed by Father Dan Hurley. 'Some fishermen and curers of Dunkelly, 1928'. From the left; Jerry O'Sullivan, Pat Dan Craher, unknown, Agnus O'Donovan, Jack Collins, unknown, Pad Danny (O'Donovan), Mikey Paul (Collins), Ricky Paul (Collins), Minni Paul (Collins) and Bridget Dwyer.
Story, 'Pat Daly and the Devil', Anon. As told by Jerry McCarthy, ‡.

September
Photograph credit, Coll., Kathleen O'Leary, 'School Photograph, 1929 - 5th, 6th and 7th year at Goleen National School'. Bottom row (from left); Nora McCarthy, Eileen Goggin, Mary Goggin, Marion O'Driscoll, Ellie

Daly, Mary Kate Donovan, Bridie Barnett, Ellen Kilganan (Lighthouse), Mary Donovan. Middle row; Tess Sullivan, Nattie Collins, Nora O'Brien, Lizzie Downey, Eileen Crowley, Ann McCarthy, Maggie Griffin, Teresa Sheehan, Nora Coughlan, Nora Goggin, Mary Scully, Kathleen McCarthy, Elizabeth Coughlan, Patricia Hamilton, Hannah Downey. Top row; Florence Driscoll, Denis McCarthy, Hubert Kilganan (lighthouse), Willie Hamilton, Michael O'Connor, Jerome Scully, Willie Canty, Willy Cotter, Tim McCarthy, Jimmy Driscoll, Mike Downey.
Photograph credit, Coll., Tess Cullinane, 'Jerry Collins'.
Story, 'The Fairies Theft', Anon., †, told by Jerry McCarthy.

October
Photograph credit, Coll., Timmy and Mary O'Sullivan, (Corran More), Threshing photographs.
Story, 'The Fire of Bones', Anon. As told by Jerry McCarthy, ‡.

November
Story, The Púca and Leprechaun, told by Jerry McCarthy.
Photograph credit, Coll., Sheila Brick, 'The McCarthy Family', Bottom Left: Julia (mother), James and Ellen. Top Left: William, William (Will the Hare) and Thomas.
Song, 'Muesheen Durkin', As sung by Julia Hodnett.
Song, 'Green Goleen', Anon. Text from Patrick P. McCarthy.
Song, 'Sailing for Americay', Anon. As sung by Denis McCarthy.
Song, 'The Parish of Sweet Kilmoe', Anon. As sung by Denis McCarthy, §.
Dhurode copper mine. 'The Abandoned Mines of West Carbery', D. Cowman and T.A. Reilly, Geological Survey of Ireland, 1988.
Song, 'Dhurode Mine', Composer Johnny Tom (O'Donovan, Mileen).
Song, 'The Hotel Song', Composed by Patrick P. McCarthy.

December
Song, 'The Turkey Buying Song', Composed by Patrick P. McCarthy.
Song, 'The Wren Day Song', Anon. Northside version.
Story, 'The Old Lady', Anon. As told by Jerry McCarthy, ‡.

Local place names for detailed fold out map

Shore names

C1	Side of Dhurode	
C3	Holes of Spureen	Holes of the rugged rocks
C4	Point of Spureen	Point of the rugged rocks
C5	Foilavilla	Cliff of the water grass
C6	Foilnamucanee	Cliff of the pigs
C7	Dhurode Beag	Small black turf
C8	Cuasawhale / Foilavisca	Cuas of the whale / watery cliff
C9	Lug of Meallán	Hollow (between headlands) of Meallán
C10	Slios	Slice or wedge
C11	Eirn Garbh	Rugged mound
C12	Cuasareca	Cove of the wreckage
C13	Hole Open	Natural arch
C14	Point of Meallán	Point of the round rocky mound
C15	Béillic of Meallán	Cavern of the round rocky mound
C16	North Point	
C17	Trágeen Abáid	Small strand of the boats
C18	Slate Quarry	
C19	South Point	
C20	Carrigcoreen	The small tapering rock
C21	Carraigaslí	Rock of the slice
C22	Pollamúislee	Hole out of the way
C23	Gareen	Small garden
C24	Speirhumber	
C25	Cuasnathoran	Cove of the thunder (noise)
C26	Lug of Gurthdove	Hollow of the black fields
C27	Carrigasceame	Rock of the steps
C28	Spar Rock	White spar rock
C29	Cuasnaglos	The green cove
C30	Peinnafearch	Point of the ravens
C31	Thunder Hole	Blow hole
C32	Cuasacopóg	Cuas of the docks (plants)
C33	Pointamór	Big point
C34	Carrig	
C35	Cuasnastaighre	Cove of the stairs
C36	Canty's Garden (Ruins)	
C37	Cuasnaghainimh	Cove of the sand
C38	Leelan / Timmy's mooring	Half land (island)
C39	Soaky Hole	
C40	Trágeen	Small strand
C41	Callue	
C42	Leighoileaunowen	Owen's grey island

C43	Carrigacuskeam	Rock of the foothold or step
C44	Leighillaun	Grey island
C45	Top of the Cuas	Top of the cove
C46	Foilabriste	Broken cliff
C47	Cuasaglór	Cuas of the noise
C48	Head of Cioun	Head of the point!
C49	Cuasanelar	Cove of the swans
C50	Red River	
C51	Lug of Dhurode	Hollow of Dhurode
C52	Lug of Dunmanus	Hollow of Dunmanus
C53	Point of Reen	Point of the headland
C54	Carrignagapull	Rock of the horse
C55	Carrigageenaclasrch	Rock with a hollow
C56	Pointaruaoileán	Point of red island
C57	Cuasgorm	Blue Cuas
C58	Bátoor	
C60	Leelan	Half land (island)
C61	Cuasabád	Broad cove
C62	Dunmanus Harbour	
C63	Cuasaneen	
C64	Cuasnamon	
C65	Cuashenlan	
C66	Tráláraigh	
C67	Trágeen	Small strand
C68	Chimney Cuas	
C69	Cuasabiní	
C70	Cuaseen Tamina	
C71	Gulí	
C72	Cuasaniscí	

Man Made Features

A1	Sheeps Cró	Sheeps small dry stone wall shelter
A2	Bone (Spring Well)	Everlasting Well
A3	Fisher's School	
A4	Burchel's Store	
A6	Bull's Cró	Bulls small dry stone wall shelter
A7	Donkey Cró	Donkeys small dry stone wall shelter
A8	Fort and souterrain	Fort and under ground chamber
A9	Rock of the Lines	
A10	Chamber	Small stone wall building for animals
A11	Killeenagh Burial Ground	
A12	Sailors Grave	
A13	Mine Hole	(Circa 1900)
A14	Famine Grave	

A15	[Dun Ceallach] (Dooneen)	
A16	Tobernasool	Well of the eyes
A26	Jackeens	Cabin ruin
A27	Black Shafteen	Mine shaft
A28	Standing Stone	
A29	Holed Stone	
A30	Canty's Ruins	
A31	Pirate Steps	
A32	Steps	
A33	Ring Fort	
A34	Cliff-edge fort	
A36	Holed Stone	
A39	Poundland	Pound (animal enclosure) Land
A40	Baile an Sagart	Priestland
A41	Well	Spring Well
A42	Well	
A43	Well	
A44	Well	
A45	Well	
A46	Well	
A47	Well	
A48	Mine Shaft	
A49	Wilkinson's Store	

Natural features

L1	Big Béillic	Big cavern
L2	Béillic of Máte	Cavern of the flat, warm place
L3	Béillic of Girrai Glos	Cavern of the green garden
L4	Béillic Te	Warm Cavern
L5	Bogabarna	Gap of the bog
L6	Gapabarna	Gap of the gap!
L9	Yellow Bog	
L10	Borhan Roadeens	Narrow road of the cow pats
L11	Cumduff	Black valley
L12	Cnonacán Mór	Big hillock
L13	Long Esc	Long small valley between steep rocks
L14	Escabarra	Narrow vally (to) the top
L15	Garibh Leaca	Rough sloping hillside
L16	Little Hill	
L17	Pollgorm	Blue Hole
L18	Lower Dhurode Ponds	
L19	Cnocán Barrfhód	Hill of the rough turf
L20	Esknastranee	Valley of the small strand
L22	Poundland Bog	

L23	Pigeon Hole	
L24	North Bottom	
L25	Big Pad's River	
L26	Meallán	The round rocky mound
L27	Bogabarra	Bog at the top
L28	Foilafreochán	Cliff of the heather
L29	Foilanáir	Cliff of the west
L30	Dunkelly Bogs	
L31	South Esc	South valley

Road names

R1	Taylors Turn	
R2	Guttery Gap / Mareens	
R3	Long Bog	
R4	Turn of Commar	Turn at the stream meeting place
R5	Bánárd Turn	Turn of the high bright place
R6	Yellow Bogs	
R7	Allan's Corner	
R8	Moss Cross	
R9	Cross of the New Road	
R10	Murphy's Turn	
R11	Turn a Barna	Turn of the gap
R12	Gap a Barna	Gap of the gap!
R13	The Cut Rock	
R14	Turn of Curly Shea	
R15	Géaracnoc	Steep hill
R15.1	Up Géaracnoc	Up the steep hill
R16	Down Meal Ramhar	Down rounded hillock
R17	Grabhaduff Turn	Rough black turn
R19	Cnonacán of a Road	Hillock of a road

Field Names

F1	Upper Lúbe	Upper twist (turn)
F2	Lower Lúbe	Lower twist (turn)
F4	Gortnabola	Field of the cattle herding
F5	Break	Rough area in a field with furze
F6	Football Field	
F7	Lower Lodge	
F8	Upper Lodge	
F9	Grafaduffs	Black grubbings
F10	Máte	Warm and flat (place)
F11	Long Ridges	
F12	Pauls Pairc Gno	Paul's busy field
F13	Killeenagh Burial Ground	Old burial ground

F16	Paircbán	White field
F18	Small Garden	
F19	Field of the Well	
F20	William's Garden	
F21	Mary Morrey's Garden	
F22	Kate's Big Field	
F23	Big Pad's Garden	
F24	Gareenamucra	The pigs small garden
F25	The Paul's Commar	Paul's at the stream meeting point
F26	The Timmy's Commar	Timmy's at the stream meeting point
F27	Paul's Pairc Gno	Paul's busy field
F28	The Curragh	The damp place
F29	The Seine Field	
F30	Well Field	
F31	Curragh	Damp place
F32	Second Curragh	
F33	Third Curragh	
F34	The Two Coals	Narrow place
F35	The Two Coals	
F36	Mangold Field	
F37	Barley Field	
F38	Long Lodge	
F39	North Lodge	
F98	Deric Field	
F99	Charity Fields	
F101	James' Sleabh	James' rough open area of grazing
F102	Willie's Paircnafarriga	Willie's field by the sea
F103	Field of the Man	
F104	Bogs - East/West	
F105	Lower Bawn	Lower enclosure
F106	Upper Bawn	Upper enclosure
F107	North Garden	
F107a	South Garden	
F107b	The Middle Garden	
F108	Sweet Fieldeen	Sweet small field
F109	The Old Field	
F111	Garranabilla	Shrubbery of the old tree
F112	Hodnett's Sleabh	Hodnett's rough open area of grazing
F113	Curraghalúbe	Damp land of the twist (turn)
F114	Outlet of Gurthdove	
F115	Pad Mickies Garden	
F116	Cnoncán na Pairc Coallea	Field of the hillock at the narrow place (ruins)
F117	Garrai Glos	Green garden
F118	Middle Meddow	

F119	Harrow Gap	
F120	Western Nub	
F121	Eastern Nub	
F122	Bawn Field	Enclosed field
F123	Garden of the Cutting	
F124	Donald's Field	
F125	Kate's Paircnagro	Kate's work field
F126	Downey's Fields	
F127	Micky's Garden	
F128	Gareen Raiserch	Little marshy garden
F129	Coalagriene	Narrow place of the sunny corner
F130	Beehive Garden	
F131	Pad the Rock Break	
F132	Mag's Garden	
F133	Big Field	
F134	Garra Beag	Small garden
F135	Leaca	Sloping hillside
F136	Pairceen	Small field
F137	The Break	The overgrown rocky place (for furze)
F138	The Long Strip	
F139	Garrainona	Turf garden
F140	Garrai Glos	Green Garden
F141	Pointe	point
F142	Downey's Sleabh	Downey's rough open area of grazing
F144	Lower Paircnacoalea	Lower (field of the ruins)
F145	Upper Paircnacoalea	Upper (field of the ruins)
F146	South Garden	
F147	Murphy's Garden	
F148	Long's Hayfield	
F149	The Two Cnoncáns	The two hillocks
F150	The Brakeen	The small overgrown rocky place for furze
F151	The Tureens	The little place for bleaching wool or flax
F152	The Tureens	The little place for bleaching wool or flax
F201	Cannart	
F202	Pairceenlean	Narrow little field
F203	Garrai Coalea	Garden of the narrow place (of the ruins)
F204	Foilbán	White cliff
F205	Upper Foilbán	Upper white cliff
F206	Garrai Cuas	Garden by the cove
F207	Football Field	
F208	Curragh Fada	Long damp place
F209	The Well Field	
F210	Shava Pairc	
F211	Garraipúca	Garden of the sprite

F212	Scraháun	Rough (scrubby) hillside
F213	Top Garden Tur	Top bleach garden
F214	Small Gardeneen Mor	The small garden (surounded by big fields)
F215	Garrailean	Narrow garden
F216	Escoinin	Little valley of the rabbits
F217	South Garden	
F218	The Long Strip	
F219	The Pairceens	The little fields
F220	Carrig Bán	White rock
F221	Big Field Tobereen	The big field of the little well
F222	Paircabarra	Top field
F223	Paircafriese	
F224	Ranu	

Further Reading

Many books and articles have been written about south-west Cork and the Mizen, which provide a general background to the area, but few refer to the Northside in detail, however, the following do give more specific detail:

'The Abandoned Mines of West Carbery', D. Cowman and T.A. Reilly, Geological Survey of Ireland, 1988.

'Shipwrecks of the Irish Coast', Edward J. Bourke, 1994.

'Canty's Cove - Legend and History', John Hawke, The Mizen Journal No. 5, 1997.

'Goleen (Kilmoe) Parish in Famine Times', Michael O'Donovan, The Mizen Journal No. 6, 1998.

'Dunmanus Castle', John Hawke, The Mizen Journal No. 7, 1999.

'An account of Local Famine Relief in the Parish of Kilmoe 1847-1848 from the John Coursey Manuscript', Mary Mackey, The Mizen Journal No. 7, 1999.

'A study of four Peninsula Parishes of West Cork 1796-1855', Rev. P. Hickey, unpublished thesis.